A Year of
INSPIRED
LIVING

Essays and Exercises for Self-Reflection

Kelly McGrath Martinsen

Health Co
Deerfield

www.hc.

Library of Congress Cataloging-in-Publication Data
is available through the Library of Congress

© 2017 Kelly McGrath Martinsen

ISBN-13: 978-07573-2009-5 (Paperback)
ISBN-10: 07573-2009-0 (Paperback)
ISBN-13: 978-07573-2005-7 (ePub)
ISBN-10: 07573-2005-8 (ePub)

HCI, its logos, and marks are trademarks of Health Communications, Inc.

Publisher: Health Communications, Inc.
         3201 S.W. 15th Street
         Deerfield Beach, FL 33442–8190

Cover design by Lawna Patterson Oldfield
Interior design and formatting by Lawna Patterson Oldfield

Contents

AUGUST

SEPTEMBER

OCTOBER

NOVEMBER

DECEMBER

*And suddenly you just know
it's time to start something new and
trust the magic of beginnings.*
—Meister Eckhart

Dear Reader:

I need your help. I can't seem to finish this book. You see, while I was writing *A Year of Inspired Living* it seemed that every time I would come to the end of a chapter I would think, *No, something is missing,* but I just didn't know what it was. Suddenly it hit me. Perhaps *I* am not meant to finish this book. Maybe—stay with me a minute—I *can't* finish this book. This is not because I am lazy, have writer's block, or because I am amazing at the art of procrastination. Nope (although all of that is true) that is not it. I think I am not able to finish this book because I am not meant to. *YOU* are! This is not just a book, it is a very specific personal, yearlong exercise created to help you live your most inspired year. Truth is, I can't write a book that tells you how to publish your life.

First, let me explain. I publish a health magazine. The mission of the magazine is to encourage people to "feel good, live simply, laugh more." That's it. Each month my job consists of picking the right articles, the right pictures, and the cover so that the entire magazine reflects that mission. I am the publisher. I love words, so I am often going to a dictionary to determine the meanings behind them. The definition of publisher was sort of vague, until that is, I found this one:

1425–75; late Middle English: "one who proclaims publicly."

It is that simple. I put the magazine together and allow it to proclaim publicly, through articles, images, and a great cover, the idea of feeling good, living simply, and laughing more. When I publish a magazine I put it all together and I write notes all over the draft. When the magazine is near completion for the month, I look at it and I contemplate it. Is it ready to publish in accordance with the mission? If so, I do the final act of writing a letter to the readers. It is called the "Letter from the Publisher" (and it is always on the first page). The letter is based on inspiration I have gleaned from the monthly articles and images and is designed to offer the readers a way to read the magazine. It tells them what articles inspire me, what images challenge me, and it hopes that the readers are inspired to maybe alter just one area of their life in that month.

Aren't you the publisher of your life? Our clothes, hair color and style; the words we choose; sports we play; diets we try; the Botox that we get or don't get (admit or don't admit)—it is all part of our personal publishing. These choices are our way of proclaiming publicly who we are. *You* are the publisher of *your life!* So wouldn't it be nice this year to solidify, via a guided writing format, your own "Letter from the Publisher"?

At the end of each week there is an area for journaling and self-reflection, but I wanted even more participation from you. I wanted this book to be self-inspiring, so I left the last week open for you, the reader, to write your own "Letter from the Publisher." As the "publisher" it is you who ultimately decides what anger you hold, what relationships you nurture, what risks you take, what wine you drink, what food you eat, what friends you keep, what God you worship, and how your life should look and feel. Share these letters, or keep them private, but engage and map out your life month by month with amazing intentions the same way a publisher maps out her magazine.

Simply put, this is a letter written to yourself that helps you to locate the things you may be searching for. It can bring to you a hearty sense of self-realization, and reveal the attributes within you that you didn't even know you possessed. This letter outlines and reminds you how you want to represent yourself, both internally and externally.

I've learned this is a powerful process. I've discovered so much about myself writing my monthly publisher letters. I discovered things I love (my wrinkles . . . could you imagine?); things I hated (muffin top . . . seriously, find me the person who is evolved enough to embrace *that*); things I was fearful about doing (surfing, parenting); and things I wanted more of (love, God, purpose).

I hope that writing these letters and journaling your reflections brings you the same joy and profound self-discovery that it brought me. If not, well then I hope you laugh at some of my silliness, cry at some of my sadness, and ultimately feel that you had a nice time sharing a confidence with a good friend.

At the end of each monthly letter that I write for the magazine, I always sign off with *Malama Pono*, which means "take care of you" in Hawaiian. That is the goal of every letter I write. That we all always take care of ourselves: mind, body, and spirit. That we feel good, live simply, and laugh more. So embark on this journey and this year, more than ever before . . .

Malama Pono,

The Process of Publishing

> Publishing is the dissemination
> of literature, music, or information —
> the activity of making information available
> to the general public.

A little more about the publisher letter, and a little bit about the layout process of the magazine, and the "layout process" of your life. I published my first letter in October 2012. This was months after I had been laid off from my job of thirteen years as a manager for a pharmaceutical company and just four weeks after I took my savings and purchased a declining health magazine and began a new career as a business owner and publisher. This career change was certainly not something advised by my accountant, my parents, or my friends, who lovingly offered these cautionary words: "The financials don't look good"; "What do you know about publishing a magazine?"; and "The timing really isn't right." They weren't entirely wrong. To compound the risk, this transition was also around the time my husband was recovering from bile duct cancer (cholangiocarcinoma), which had meant months of chemo plus radiation, followed by a liver transplant, and then many years of multiple surgeries to correct initial surgical errors. It was also just six years after my son had recovered from Landau-Kleffner syndrome, a rare epileptic disorder. To say the years prior to my involuntary career change (a polite way of saying I was canned) had been busy would be an understatement. To say those years reshaped my entire view on life, well that would be dead on!

The very first letter I wrote that bright September day was one that talked about risk-taking. I could speak about this from experience. I was walking away from a career that I'd started in my early twenties, one that I had been good at and had quickly become tied to my identity. I climbed that corporate ladder with a promotion every three years and was on a fast track to becoming an executive. Yet once I was let go, I made the decision that I could live without the big salary, without the company car (that kinda hurt), without the sales trips, and even without the accolades and promotions that pharmaceutical companies are famous for handing out. What I could not live without—or so I thought—was being busy. I don't think I'd even considered slowing down because *I couldn't*. I couldn't "breathe and be present" because I was working on my laptop while drinking old coffee in hospital waiting rooms. If I wasn't there, I was making quick calls home from airports to see how everyone was doing. I didn't know it yet, but when I was "downsized"—even after all the years of blood, sweat, and sacrifice—the jackass who lowered the boom was really providing me a "get out of jail free" pass.

Back to writing. I had written as a form of private therapy since I was a child. After reading an essay I had written, my fourth-grade teacher Mrs. Schnide commented, "You will be a great poet! Or inspire one." (Everyone should be lucky enough to have a Mrs. Schnide in their life). At Holy Trinity High School, Mr. McCloud asked, "Have you considered journalism for a career?" after grading one of my more sarcastic writing pieces. The truth is, no I had not. Writing was my secret weapon; it was simply for me, to be shared *only* when I needed an A! So I was a little tickled but somewhat nervous to write that very first Letter from the Publisher. I was writing what was akin to an inspiration piece—and it was fun.

After what I'd been through, I found these letters were a form of self-therapy. While I was writing for my readers, in all honesty, my real audience was . . . me. I was talking to myself, going through the life stresses I had experienced over the last few years, and basically reminding myself that, while it wasn't the life path I had expected, I was surviving. I expanded my writing, with observations on my own experiences and observations on humanity.

When I wrote, I didn't imagine that anyone—except for maybe my mom—was reading the letters (which is silly, the magazine had a readership of 55,000 people). Still, I was genuinely surprised when, within two days of the first issue of the magazine hitting the stands, my phone rang with a call from a woman who *loved* my letter—and it wasn't my mom! I should mention here that while I wrote this first letter in September 2012, the first issue didn't hit the streets until that October, and this call came in on October 26. I was actually in tears when I answered the phone. I had just taken this huge financial risk by sinking an enormous amount of money into starting a new career and building a nice office in my basement. I was ready to take on the world, but Mother Nature had other plans. This was when Hurricane Sandy—at the time the second costliest storm in United States history—decided to barrel through Long Beach, New York, leaving a third of my home, all of my office, and a large portion of my town flooded in four feet of sewage, sand, and seawater.

The woman on the other end of the phone began, "Hi, I am really sorry to call you, I didn't think the phone call would go through but I am sitting here on a two-hour long gas line and I remembered I had your magazine in my car.[1] So I was sitting in my car on line and I realized I had picked up your magazine so that I had something to read while I waited and I opened it to your letter," her voice broke a little and I could her start to sniffle. "I guess I just want to say thanks, I loved it! It spoke to me, and you know, just thank you, you are right." She hung up quickly, and I never had a chance to ask her what I was right about.

---

1. Days after the storm devastated Long Island, gas was almost nonexistent. People needed gas not only for their cars but also to run generators since the power was out in all of our towns for days, or even weeks in some areas. When gas stations did get fuel, the lines would stretch for miles.

It turned out it didn't matter what I was "right" about because what connected with her was not what connected with others. That phone call indicated two things to me: first, my written form of "self-therapy" was being read by more people than just my parents, and second, you should definitely pick up the free magazines in your yoga studios and grocery stores because you never know when you may get stuck in a two-hour gas line and need something to read!

There were times when I was overwhelmed by writing the letter. A month would fly by and I would think, *Really? You need another letter already?* I would panic, become agitated, and literally decide that I would rather sell this magazine then try and think of a topic to write about. I gave myself a trick. As a reader and a writer I am in love with the English language, so I made it simple: I would look to find inspiration or contemplation on what was happening in my life and I would not require myself to write a whole letter; I would simply choose a word—hope, love, inspiration, selfless—and then I would write from there.

I continued to write these letters each month, inspired by a quote, a news event, an event in my own life, a song, a memory, a word, whatever. The letters covered a range of topics including wellness, conscious eating, fitness, environment, love, self-discovery. I even wrote a letter about dog crap (come on people, pick it up!). I also continued to receive calls and emails each month. Not everyone loved the letters (check out the call I got in July). But most of the calls and emails were positive: "Great letter," "Thank you," "You really reached me." I began to see that while we are all adults and we all inherently know what should be valued, more often than not, we forget. Too often we become busy and the reminders of who we want to be and how we want to love become Post-it notes that are stuck up on our vision boards, or Pinterest boards, or shared on Facebook only to be forgotten minutes later.

The hope for this book is that you read it (obviously), though not all at once in the same manner I have been known to gorge myself on leftover birthday cake. No, because while no one loves a binge (cake, book, or Netflix series) more than me, binging won't work with this book. Instead *A Year of Inspired Living* should be read slowly, one letter a week, and savored more like a fine wine. I have left a blank page after each month for you to experiment. Ideally, you won't just read this book, you will write it! There is ample room for you to write notes and reflections after each week. After you complete reading those three topic weeks, the fourth week, well, that is up to you. Write your publisher letter! Want to be really spunky? Take a real risk and put your letter up on *www.ayearofinspiredliving.com* and share it with everyone (nothing vulgar, folks).

One caveat: there is a fine line between self-help and bullsh*t. I do my best to keep the BS at a minimum. I tell you only what I tell myself. If you find you are reading what you think might be BS, stop judging and remember, these letters are from me to me and shared with you. It is my publisher letter to myself. They are precisely what I deemed necessary for *me*. There may be other times when you read a letter and it completely resonates (score!), and times when you may disagree wholeheartedly. That's okay, too, that is what your pages are for. Write *your* letter!

A Year of Inspired Living [2] is filled with teachings. You've probably heard the saying, "Those who *can't,* teach." I don't always agree with that, but in this case there is some truth. I in no way want my readers to think these letters come from a higher place. I don't know more than you and I haven't spent five years on an ashram focused on self-discovery. Although I search, I haven't spoken to God; I am quite simply an everyman, focused on self-improvement . . . *my self.* My letters are *my* therapy, *my* reminder that I need to quiet my "internal crazy" and force myself to live an inspired life. The overwhelming response that I have received to these letters indicate to me that ya'll got some crazy you want to quiet as well! I hope this book helps you on this journey and that with the guidance placed in here you live your most inspired year ever!

---

2. *Perhaps you have learned about this book in August, not in January where the book starts. NO PROBLEM! Simply start in the month you picked it up and go from there. The first chapter does not dictate the beginning, it is dictated by YOUR first engagement.*

Intentions

riting is an essential part of this journey and here is where we start engaging. In the space below, write your own intentions for this book. If you are reading an eBook, certainly you can swipe up to the notes section and place your notes there, or grab a beautiful companion journal or a simple spiral notebook and pen and keep it by your reading space.

_____

_____

_____

_____

_____

_____

_____

_____

_____

_____

_____

_____

_____

_____

_____

_____

January

Can you remember who you were
before the world told you
who you should be?

−Danielle LaPorte

RESOLUTIONS

*I don't mean to brag but . . .
I finished my 14-day diet in
3 hours and 12 minutes.*

Resolution: *A firm decision to do or not to do something.*

"My name is Kelly and I am a resolution-making failure."
"HELLO KELLY!" Aha, good, I see I am not alone!
A few years back on January 1, I gave up sugar as a New Year's resolution. Unfortunately, on January third I was found eating a tub of Ben and Jerry's Fish Food . . . with a side of Christmas cookies. In fairness, I did feel I needed to rid the house of all temptation—easier to do it in one fell swoop! Another January, I joined a gym with a lifetime membership, pledging to go five times a week. Yes, I still have the membership; no I haven't been there in over ten months. But this past January I figured it out. Forget body, let's work on the spirit—that's something I can stick to! So I started the free twenty-one-day meditation recordings with Oprah and Deepak Chopra. Honestly, this meditation was so amazing, I mean it was literally *life-transforming*! Well, it was, at least for four of the twenty-one days that I actually listened to the recordings.

Ugh! New Year's resolutions! If you are like me, you start January with a bang. You are doing everything you know you should be doing, you are journaling your reflections, juicing or blending your green smoothies, heading to the gym after work, and scheduling a calendar full of time with friends, family, and even date nights with your significant other. If you are also like me, by the tenth of January, you find yourself discouraged by the winter produce that's available in your grocery store, so you begin exchanging green drinks at the farmers market for café lattes at Starbucks. By the twenty-first, you will probably deem that January offers an entirely unacceptable degree of coldness in the air (oh, yes, even people in Florida are known to do this) and find that instead of meeting up with friends for dinner, you would rather binge-watch episodes of *Friends* on Netflix (while also binging on a nice bowl of ice-cream). Sadly, by the beginning of February, your favorite spin or kick-boxing instructor has left your gym or yoga studio and the replacement instructor actually makes you viscerally angry because he/she doesn't instruct the participants to do enough sit-ups (*jeez!*). Or worse, that new instructor expects you to do entirely *too many* sit-ups (is Mrs. Perfect Body kidding me?). This frustration allows you to believe that it is not only in *your* best interest that you skip class but also in the new instructor's best interest that you forgo the class.

Is this what we have come to? Are we quitters? Are we often lazy, sometimes apathetic, ridiculously overwhelmed, and do we use these excuses to be quitters? Well, yeah, I guess I do. I see you smiling so I think you do, too. ☺

This year, my only resolution is to be resolute! If I take something on—like scheduling a space each month to organize—then I will stick with it. Being a serial "resolution failure," you may ask how I plan on achieving this resoluteness. For me, it truly comes down to smaller goals. As good as a year membership at a gym looks, I know myself; I get bored or things change. I have recently taken up purchasing class cards on Groupon versus yearlong or lifetime memberships. This allows me to try things first. I can take the time to feel the vibe of the studio/gym and then choose my poison. (Yes, most often I view physical exercise as poison.) All kidding aside though, exercise is modern medicine and it will keep you healthy and strong. Yes, I know this for a fact. So rather than focusing on having the resolution to achieve six-pack abs by summer (which would be really awesome), make your goals smaller. Perhaps, just do enough core work to simply alleviate some of your back pain. Or maybe even smaller, surely we can carry more grocery bags in from the car each week, or carry a child (or puppy) for longer periods of time. Choosing the stairs over the elevator . . . that's a classic, we know it! But are we doing it? This January I will! (And I hope you will, too).

Don't want to place physical activity on your resolution list? I get it. What about the age-old "diet/eating healthy" resolution? Most of my Januarys have been spent tossing everything white (sugar, flour, etc.) into the garbage. February, I am back in the grocery store purchasing . . . you got it, sugar, flour, etc. Many health gurus swear by the brilliant idea of eating a diet that is 70 percent "whole food," or food that is as close to its original state as possible. That seems manageable because it leaves 30 percent wiggle room for reality (reality is also known as sugar, flour, etc.).

This January you may have already begun to be more resolute; you have this book and with it the ability to journal your goals and dreams for the next twelve months. Stick with it, write your life chapters, take small goals and knock them out of the park! Go ahead, pick a small resolution and then stick to it! Fall off track in February. Well, hell, isn't that what February is for? "Fall off February," "Failure February," whatever you call it, try and avoid it. But, if it catches you off guard and you find yourself on the couch, remote in one hand, cookies in the other, forgive yourself—failure happens. Except this year be different, be resolute, but also be resilient and recognize that one failure is not a reason to quit entirely.

Failure is simply a reason to try again. So forgive yourself for the small failures and encourage yourself to continue on the path of greater health. The new year always offers within it a form of forgiveness and a nice place to start over! Here is your new beginning. Your year is a 365-page book—write a good one!

Reflections

WHAT ARE YOUR RESOLUTIONS THIS YEAR?

LIVING

*You don't have to find out
you are dying to start living.*
—Zach Sobiech

Living: *Not dead; having life. Currently active.*

We are not guaranteed a long, healthy, or easy life. I mean, certainly we can do things to protect ourselves. We can choose to eat foods that are GMO-free, organic, and as close to their natural state as possible. We can choose to run, surf, hike, bike ride, practice yoga, or meditate, all in an effort to lower our stress levels and keep our bodies strong. (It has only been a week. Please tell me you are keeping up with your healthy lifestyle resolution choices!) ☺ Yet even with all these good lifestyle choices, we cannot predict the day that will be our last. Imagine if you were able to know the date that you would die. Imagine it was looming on a calendar. Would you live your life differently?

Tim McGraw's song "Live Life Like You're Dying" describes, in his perfect Southern twang, what the fictional character of his song did when he learned he had only months to live. He jumped out of an airplane, climbed the Rockies, rode on a bull named Blue Manchu, and was quick to love and forgive.

A cynic may say, "Sure, you can do that if you are dying, but if you aren't dying, there are mortgages, rent, taxes, literally a *stack* of dishes in the sink that need washing, and a world of obligations that can stop you from riding a bull or climbing a mountain." I agree it isn't realistic to do all of these things (bummer, I had my eyes on Blue Manchu). ☺ But come on, we can do *some* of it. We can stop saying "no" and maybe force ourselves to say, "yes" once in a while. Yes to something new. Yes to signing up to run a race. Yes to meeting a friend for dinner on a specific date each month. Yes to taking a bike ride with your kids every Sunday. The dishes in the sink? They'll wait for you (if your family is anything like mine, I can *guarantee* they'll wait for you). The bills, they'll still be there waiting to be paid.

Here is the truth, and believe me it isn't easy for me to tell you this, but you do need to know . . . you *are* dying. You might be thinking, "Dying? I don't even have a cold!" Yet, every day you live brings you one day closer to your death. So with that cheery thought in the front of your mind I recommend making a list. No, not a bucket list (although that is fun, too). No, a list of wishes and dreams. This list should be a bit different than a bucket list because the purpose is not to create a list to cross things off until you are left with a list of scratched-out items and time on your hands. Nope, create a list that *grows with you*. Because as we hurl toward our impending demise, the truth is *it should be fun!* And it should be ever-changing. What was "fun" for me in my twenties, isn't so fun anymore (wearing a bikini)! ☺

Seriously, I wanted to be an actress starting at age four. Around the time of my fortieth birthday, after working on some TV shows (Google Sally Kellerman *Ghost Stories* and you can see my debut), I decided that acting wasn't for me—right now. It didn't get scratched off my list, I just added more things to the list. I wasn't giving up a dream. My life can change, and one day I will want to act again. Is acting on your list? Go to your local community theater and audition. If you don't get the part, offer to work behind the scenes and then audition for the next one . . . and the next. Find it's not for you? Keep it on your list and gracefully move on to your next "Blue Manchu."

You know what I discovered was for me? Stand-up paddle surfing in head-high waves! I promise you, in a million years I *never* thought that would be for me; for a huge part of my life I was afraid of the ocean! But right now, you can't get me out of the ocean (even in the winter in New York). It took time, going out on the flattest of days, riding small little ripples back to the shore, challenging myself to face a fear and reminding myself that I don't have forever to learn this. You don't either.

Speaking sweeter? Loving deeper? How can you *not* have time for that? YOU ARE DYING! It sucks, but now you know. So make yourself a "Living Wish List," not once but a thousand times! Let it evolve, let yourself experience some of it and forgo some of it. Add new stuff and delete old stuff and then see what transpires for you. This is your wish list. I wish I surfed, acted, spent more time reading. I wish I was nicer, was more fastidious, more resolute, ate more ice-cream (gasp), spoke more calmly to my teenagers (hey I didn't say this list was easy). I wish, I wish, I wish. Make your list, filled with loving intentions, badass fear, concurring goals and wishes, and let it change. Remember, you aren't married to it.

The truth is, the day I die I would love nothing more than for my family to see a list of dreams on the refrigerator and a bunch of dirty dishes in the sink. How about you?

Here is a peek at my list (honestly, my real one is like five pages and growing):

- Call your parents (remember they are dying, too ☹)
- Blue Manchu (I had to!)
- Start every morning greeting my family members with "I love you!"
- See "my girls" at least every four months
- Get back to family vacations in the Outer Banks—that time, those memories, were everything
- Zip line (did it once, deathly afraid to do it again . . . so do it again)
- Ride "The Hulk" at Universal (children do not read this and badger me to take you to Universal . . . seriously)

- Surf in South America
- Travel Europe with the kids
- Travel Europe (with just Kevin)
- Spend more time at the beach (you live here for a reason!)
- Buy a second home (rent it for income?)
- Write and publish a book (hell yeah, that's getting crossed off)
- Write another book
- Act
- Contain your self-pride at your child's sporting events (while I do this, I am so close to crying with joy when these spunky kids hit their own goals)
- Date nights (seriously, I don't care if you are tired, cranky, or your husband is grating on your very last nerve; go to dinner, a movie, a show, a beach walk—just go)
- Girls' weekend (you will be surprised at how well your family survives without you)
- Be easy breezy from time to time; ice-cream for kids' dinner and maybe even breakfast ☺

Reflections

WHAT IS YOUR LIVING WISH LIST?

_____
_____
_____
_____
_____
_____
_____
_____
_____
_____
_____
_____
_____
_____
_____
_____
_____
_____
_____
_____
_____
_____
_____
_____

NARCISSISM

*People are often unreasonable and self-centered.
Forgive them anyway. If you are kind, people
may accuse you of selfish, ulterior motives. Be kind
anyway. If you are honest people may cheat you.
Be honest and sincere anyway. If you find happiness,
people may be jealous. Be happy anyway. The good you
do today may be forgotten tomorrow. Do good anyway.
Give the world the best you have and it may never
be enough. You're your best anyway. For you see,
in the end, it is between you and God.
It was never between you and them anyway.*

—Mother Teresa

Narcissism: *The misguided belief that everything is about you.*

My favorite part of this quote from Mother Teresa is where she says, "For you see, in the end, it is between you and God. It was never between you and them anyway."

We all react. Example: you are driving down the road singing Taylor Swift's "Shake It Off" at the top of your lungs when some man-child who looks like he should be driving a Big Wheel instead of a car crosses the yellow line into your lane. You react. For me, my reaction often starts with my middle finger or a firm hand pressing maniacally on my horn. Sometimes, it is a finger with one hand, horn with the other. You may even forget he is just a teenager and curse him as a "Horrible excuse for a human being."

Along with the road hazards, our reactivity is also challenged by social media. For instance, you see on Facebook that your daughter's friend had five girls over for a sleepover and your daughter was left off the guest list. Your reaction is to hit the passive-aggressive "LIKE" button, thinking smugly, *I "liked" this to let you know I do not LIKE this.*

When it comes to our family members we usually react because we believe we know the motives behind their actions. We often think to ourselves that we have known these sisters, brothers, cousins, parents our whole lives; of course, we know why they do the things they do!

Our belief that we know and understand the driving factors that are the catalysts within our relationships, though, is often not based on the reality of the situation. The belief we hold about the driver of the car that cut me off is that he is some hotshot teenager with his first car, and "he was probably texting" (Wow, I just sounded like my mother!). Your belief about the mom on Facebook is that she is a show-off; she wants to shove her perfect family in everyone's face. And your family . . . oh, you know your family's driving factors. Or do you?

I bet you would be surprised to know that these beliefs are just that— *your* beliefs. It is human nature to judge another person by his or her actions; it is also human nature to assign our own internal meaning to those actions. Nine times out of ten, our assigned meanings are incorrect.

Back to that nut that cut me off. You are right, he is an egotistical teenager, but the fact was he was also running to the hospital to see his grandpa one last time. And "Mrs. Perfect Facebook"—that "friend" of yours with the photos of her perfect child at the perfect sleepover that your daughter wasn't invited to? Well, you see, those photos are not really intended for you; they are for her. They remind her how blessed she is when times are tough, and she's been having a lot of those tough times lately. You see her mother is dying and her husband works too much (at least that's where he says he is) and this mom feels completely dissatisfied and unappreciated at home. When she posts those pictures of her child's birthday, she is sharing the joys in her life, and hoping that the number of "likes" she gets on these pictures validate her choice of giving up her career so that she could raise her children, or validate her for hosting a successful party even though she is not a stay-at-home mother. The truth is, she works a sixty-hour week and barely knew these children before tonight. She is so caught up in her own problems, that inviting or not inviting your child never crossed her mind. The party, the lack of an invitation, even her social media post—had *nothing* to do with you. Oh, and your family member whose motives you know so well because you lived together all your life? Well, honestly, you don't. You don't know what motivates him or her anymore. You haven't lived in the same house in over ten, twenty years, maybe more. You no longer know what motivates your sister (or friend) when she makes bad choices; how could you? Instead of assuming that you know why she is doing something, why not ask her? How about your high school friend who has "always been _____" (seriously you could fill that blank in with any word you like, crazy, slutty, selfish, annoying, needy) you don't know why she is acting out in life at this moment in her late forties, just because you remember how she was in high school.

Why not take a minute to question a behavior rather than judge it. Recognize that more likely than not it has nothing to do with you. Clarify, understand, or, better yet, just offer your fellow "man" the benefit of the doubt. As humans, we just don't do that enough with one another. Our natural response is to pass judgment.

Let's stop passing judgment on one another's actions and stop assigning our own interpreted meaning to those actions. Instead, when we find ourselves in a situation and things happen and two paths cross leaving you feeling annoyed or unhappy, and you find yourself judging another person's self-centered motives, recognize instead that these actions more than likely have less than nothing to do with you. As Mother Teresa said, "It was never between you and them anyway."

Reflections

IT WAS NEVER BETWEEN YOU AND
_____ ANYWAY*

Perhaps list here people to whom you should be kinder, or to whom you should give the benefit of the doubt; simply recognize their actions are not about you.

_____
_____
_____
_____
_____
_____
_____
_____
_____
_____
_____
_____
_____
_____
_____
_____
_____
_____
_____

YOUR VERY FIRST
"PUBLISHER'S LETTER"

Imagine you are the publisher of your own magazine. Write a letter to your audience, yourself. Your "Publisher's Letter" can be based on one, all, or none of the topics we touch on each month. Need help? For me, I start with an observation or something I did this month, so perhaps you can, too.

WE INTERRUPT THIS CHAPTER TO DO A QUICK CHECK-IN

My alone time is sometimes for your safety.

Your first month is finished. What did you think? Did you read three weeks all at once? Week-by-week? Did you write notes? Write a "Publisher Letter" to yourself? If yes, great! Together, we will work on living a more inspired life. If not, go back. Take a cup of coffee (or a glass of wine!) and hide somewhere away from the kids, the dog, the too-long to-do list, and work you brought home from the office. Sit down and write letters to yourself, evaluate your resolutions, your perceptions, and the things you want more of in your life. Freely put pen to paper (or fingers to keyboard) and see what flows. Also feel free to share your experience at *ayear ofinspiredliving.com* or #AYOIL.

INSPIRATION STATION

se this page to brainstorm topic ideas or even doodle. Let this be your creative space to let your mind run free.

February

February,
I know you will
be fabulous!

VAINGLORY

Vainglory: *Excessive elation or pride over one's own*
achievements. Boastful vanity.

O scar Wilde once said, "The consciousness of loving and being loved brings a warmth and richness to life that nothing else can bring." Amen! Don't you just love, love? The month of February is often described as a "love" month. The idea of love is historically defined as a feeling or exchange of intense emotion shared between two (oh, how I love definitions!). Love could be thought of as an exchange between two people, a person and a pet, or in some cases a person and an object (yes, I love my Louis Vuitton wallet!)—but always two. Is this necessary? Is it even fair to the concept of love to say that you can only feel it or achieve it as part of a pair? Because to be honest you only need yourself to experience the warmth Oscar Wilde defines. In fact, it is easier to share love between two people if you first love one person—yourself. Sound cliché? Maybe it is to some degree, but it is also true. Because to love someone, you must know how to love through imperfections—and we all have them.

I didn't always subscribe to this "self-love" talk. Seriously, you don't have to look further than a self-help book, church, a yoga class, or a social media meme to realize self-love is all the rage. Still, even with these constant reminders, I didn't really embrace or vibe with the whole "self-love revolution" until one day when there was a slight change in my daily routine. Truth is, I first came to recognize the value of self-love because my imperfect ass was running behind schedule!

I was late to yoga class, and I had to place my mat in a space that was not my usual spot. This started me off feeling very unsettled. I *loved* my yoga space. I felt strong in that yoga space. I obtained headstand in that space. I had a partnership with that space. My space and I had an unspoken agreement: if I was there in that space, taking that class, then I would achieve new poses, or stay longer in difficult poses or even just have the best Savasana of my life. (Savasana means "rest" and many yoga classes end with it; who doesn't want to have the best rest of their life?) But I was late, and some woman had *her* yoga mat in *my* space. So while I eyed the woman and her JadeYoga mat that were sitting in my beautiful space with a jealousy so strong it was verging on rage, I walked quickly to a new space. As if the idea that I had a new space wasn't bad enough, the only spot available at the studio came with something so horrific that I began making my way to the exit. The yoga teacher saw me and guided me gently back to that horrific spot. What was there that made me almost bolt for the door? *A mirror!*

When I do downward dog, I usually feel strong. Core sucked in, shoulder blades tucked in my back pockets, hands spread wide; I *love* my downward dog, always have. Today though, the view I got in that mirror was not the same view I had held in my mind. No, the reality was the view in the mirror: a forty-seven-year-old ass. I was horrified, thinking about the miles I run, the effort I make to eat right—and in the end *this* is what my downward dog (read ass) *really* looks like? I was in a tizzy, I couldn't hold a pose to save my life, I was seriously unsteady and found myself wobbling in mountain pose. (Mountain pose is basically standing up straight.)

After what seemed like forever, this mirror-dominated class was finally coming to a close and I realized that I had spent the past hour chastising myself for my food mishaps, blaming my mother for my genes and the big hips that come with them, and then berating myself for my "un-evolved vanity." When I finally went into the closing pose of the series, headstand pose, the face looking back at me in the mirror not only didn't look strong, it looked funny. Really funny, like, "wrinkles upside down" funny.

It looked so funny that I stood there and I laughed. Literally, I laughed out loud, undoubtedly killing the Zen of several of my class-mates. I laughed at my fat ass, my focus, my wrinkles, and my vanity. And right then I loved myself. I had wasted the last hour judging myself on the things that I try never to judge others: the clothes I was wearing, the weight on my hips, the upside down muffin top (really, a muffin top is bad enough right side up, but upside down the view is indescribable). It was only when I looked at my wrinkles, which looked even worse when turned topsy-turvy, that I finally had the opportunity to smile. With the smile came the laugh and with that laugh I thought, *You're funny, Kelly. I love you!*

We all do it, though, don't we? Our thighs are too big, our lips too thin, the roots of our hair are too dark or too light. We stand in judgment of ourselves instead of providing the same love that we offer our friends and family.

Every morning, why don't you (and I) make an effort to focus on falling in love with yourself! It is a real challenge to love yourself with the same abandon as you love a child, a pet, a partner, or a designer handbag. If you focus on your strengths, on the things you *can* do instead of what you *can't* do—like maybe squeeze into your old swimsuit ☺—you may just realize how lovable you are. I can do a handstand (after practicing for three years) and I love myself for it (even if my face looks funny upside down). When I love myself I am a better mom, a better sister, daughter, wife, and friend—and in return I become more lovable to everyone in my life. When I love myself, I am the person I *want* to be. Loving yourself is not being complacent or automatically accepting. It is often the opposite. When you truly love yourself, sometimes you must change your attitude, your food choices, your relationship choices.

Loving and being in love should start with you! When it does, you begin to make the right choices and fill the world with your own light. That light reflects out to the universe and brings you loving partnerships. It comes full circle. Every day is a new beginning with new decisions to make. When we wake up each morning we can either spend fifteen minutes recognizing some wonderful things that we love about ourselves and even writing them down on the next page. Or we can spend fifteen minutes digging through the closet to find the pair of pants that make us look skinny! (Stop hitting the snooze button and you can do both!) But the truth is, if we forgo those fifteen minutes of skinny-pants searching, we just might be on time for yoga!

Reflections

WHAT DO YOU LOVE ABOUT YOURSELF?

_____

_____

_____

_____

_____

_____

_____

_____

_____

_____

_____

_____

_____

_____

_____

_____

_____

_____

_____

_____

_____

_____

LOVE

*Falling in love is easy . . . but staying
in love is very special!*

Love: *A feeling of strong or constant regard for
and dedication to someone.*

Okay, so we talked about love, you have written a list about all the things you love about yourself. *Yippee!* But you don't want this book to become sickeningly Pollyanna-ish, so I am going to share something with you that I hate. I hate Valentine's Day! Reading that sentiment, you may conclude I've never been in love, I'm going through a relationship shift, or I'm just a miserable person; however, you'd be wrong. I'm actually married to a man I love a good 98 percent of the time (the remaining 2 percent, I'm busy deciding where to hide the body). I am not miserable. Actually, I am pretty happy because I believe life is a blessing. But, as happy as I am, I am also realistic and I have come to learn that life, even a blessed one, is anything but perfect. Valentine's Day proves it.

My strong negative feelings toward Valentine's Day have to do with the fact that this holiday pretends life or, more accurately, love is "perfect" at its inception. I contend that things often *seem* perfect. I go further and say that what seems perfect is often *not* perfect; it is just a first-time experience. There is a difference between perfect and new. Valentine's Day reminds us of new, of firsts: first date, first kiss, first apartment, first trip, first child. Sure, the first kiss is great (hopefully the first child, too)! Everyone knows that, but *why* is it great? Because it's new! When love is new it has the wonderful added energy of anticipation and discovery, "Wow you like the Beatles? ME TOO!" However, anticipation and discovery are not love. Anticipation is excitement. Anticipation is an endorphin high. The first kiss isn't love! Waking up and kissing each other when you're ninety-eight years old for the 100 billionth time (and the breath that goes with it!)—*that's* love! And love, well it takes work!

In my opinion true love is watching someone floss their teeth and kissing them right after, or even worse sitting on a toilet while they floss their teeth and then days or even minutes later being intimate with that same person. And real love is doing that over and over and over. Trust me, and I say this with all due respect to my husband, saying "I love you" is a lot easier *before* you've shared a bathroom. Real love often means putting up with each other's crappy (no pun intended) behavior and forgiving each other for being imperfect. True love is rediscovering each other again and again and again. And when you are angry or, worse, find yourself becoming indifferent to the person you are with, love is the energy you will need to make you go deeper and share an even more profound level of yourself, a side of you the person you are with has never seen.

In Liane Moriarty's novel *The Husband's Secret*, she writes of a couple that is struggling with a choice: "They could fall in love with fresh, new people, or they could have the *courage and humility* to tear off some essential layer of themselves and reveal to each other a whole new level of *otherness*, a level far beyond what sort of music they each liked." Wow! Stripping down layers of you, revealing a new level of "otherness," and falling in love with a different aspect of the same person year after year. That is probably what St. Valentine had in mind. That would take humility, courage, patience—and it's a risk! Yes, to show someone a new part of you is a risk!

The key word in that definition of love above is *constant!* Love needs to be constant. I remember how I felt when I met my husband at twenty years old; I couldn't *not* think about him, his wavy hair, his muscles, and his cute, sly grin. Twenty-year-old me had an ongoing fairy tale with twenty-year-old him. I miss twenty-year-old me. She had so many admirable qualities. The Kelly that Kevin first fell in love with was fun! She had no fear; she had endless energy; no wrinkles and—yup, you guessed it—she had perky boobs!

I imagine sometimes my husband misses her, too. (And not just her boobs.) You see, forty-seven-year-old me can sometimes be a hot mess: forgetting to breathe during her son's wrestling match or her daughter's lacrosse game; stressing over the last bill that came in the mail; and snapping at her children or her husband when she is on a business call. Some days she might be too tired and stressed to remember to even kiss her husband goodnight. Forty-seven-year-old me sort of sucks sometimes. Or at least she is not nearly as fun as twenty-year-old me. That's okay because guess what? My forty-seven-year-old husband is not his twenty-year-old-self either (hello, hair loss). We can't be, we have responsibilities; worse, we have *shared* responsibilities. If you think paying bills or caring for a loved one is hard alone, just wait until there are two of you making the decisions. For me and Kevin—together for twenty-seven years total—more ups than downs; but, yes, downs.

When we reach those down times in relationships, we need to stop avoiding, and to spend some time with one another and rediscover those areas of compatibility we had when we first met (pre kids, mortgages, bosses, fat asses, and hair loss). I'll bet that whatever made you both laugh twenty years ago still makes you laugh now, even with all your individual "evolution." Put faith and stock in the fact that, since you are still together decades later, you are still compatible. But don't let that be it. Compatibility cannot be the end goal. You must use your compatibility as a match that lights the flame of chemistry between your souls.

You *must* have chemistry. You cannot be too tired, or too busy, or too anything that you forgo the chemistry. Chemistry (read s-e-x) is vital at age twenty, forty, sixty, even ninety! Don't just take my word for it. If you sigh as you are reading this, realizing you are in a completely compatible but spark-free relationship, light a flame! Buy some sexy lingerie or just have a "quickie" to see how much closer you are when you are intimate. Notice afterward that you care just a little less about dirty dishes in the sink. Recognize how much less you fight or get on each other's nerves! It may take work and might not be spontaneous, unlike the people in those commercials with the twin bathtubs; you may have to make it an appointment on your calendar. Still, I say do it . . . yes do *it*. ☺

Existing in a long-term relationship, romantic or otherwise, should be the thing that makes our heart race. Yet, so often the endorphins win out. I have seen it time and again. A couple decides to end a relationship because it is easier to be excited by someone new than courageously share a new part of himself or herself.

It may be trivial, but I often think of spouses like cars. I maintain that if you are lusting for this new, hot car, just because it looks like it's fast or sharp or whatever, don't buy it until you are positive you have kicked the tires on your old car. Take a risk and see if you can bring that car to new speeds, appreciate the memories within that old car's fading leather, remember the hopes and the dreams you had when you first bought it, and then check the engine. The truth is you haven't learned everything there is to learn about your old car. Take a look under the hood and discover that the person you already think you know everything about has more layers than you could examine in ten lifetimes. Find out what has changed within them while you were busy having careers and raising kids. Take a moment, reconnect, share your changes, and fall in love again and again, year after year. Then, for you, Valentine's Day will be more than one day in February.

Reflections

REMIND YOURSELF HOW HOT YOUR SIGNIFICANT OTHER IS.

(Or skip this entire writing section and meet your spouse at the door naked!)

MANIFEST

Manifest: *Clear or obvious to the eye or mind.*

only recently became aware of something called the Law of Attraction. Crazy, right? That is the entire premise of the bestselling book *The Secret*. But at the time that book came out, life was great for me, I didn't need a book. I figured that whatever the secret in *The Secret* was, I must already know it because I was happy. Ah, yes, your young adult years can be almost fairy-tale-like can't they? Fast forward toward middle age . . . I learn about a conference and my magazine is asked to sponsor it. The focus of the conference? Yup, you got it, the Law of Attraction. I am going to tell you a little about the theory and then I'll share my experience with it. Then I think you should come to your own conclusions about it.

It's funny, when I looked up the Law of Attraction, the word "pseudoscience" was one of the first things to pop up:

*In the New Thought philosophy, the **law of attraction** is the belief that by focusing on positive or negative thoughts a person brings*

*positive or negative experiences into their life. . . . **Law of attraction** is*
an example of a pseudoscience.

More simply said, "Like always attracts like."

First, I want to clarify that the Law of Attraction (LOA) intrigues me,
not as a science but perhaps more as a general rule. So the "pseudoscience" label doesn't' bother me. This book isn't a science experiment and
neither is your life. So let's turn away from that argument and move forward. Deep believers of the LOA state that you need not take any action
toward your goal; it is simply your thoughts that allow the Universe to
grant you your abundance or your lack thereof. I say your thoughts (and
mine, too) are worthless without action. The LOA at its core states that if
you want to *be* successful, you *act* successful. From my understanding of
it, the LOA says one must behave *as if* you already have the goal. I don't
know if I believe that.

I want to share with you two LOA anecdotes. As publisher of a magazine, I encounter tons of people every day. One particular guy, whom
I will call Rob, was a devotee of the LOA, and his dream was to help
others discover it and become a self-help guru. Rob wanted to be the
next Tony Robbins. He self-published a book and from that point on
he acted like he had already hit the mark. He stopped speaking to me
directly and instead had an assistant call me. When we finally met face-
to-face at an expo, he was traveling with a PR person, who acted as his
mouthpiece even though he was standing right next to her. He and I
were speaking, for instance, and she would interrupt and say, "What Rob
needs from your magazine is . . . " as though Rob wasn't standing inches
away and couldn't think or talk for himself. The second person who also
traveled with Rob was a photographer who would snap pictures as if he
were already famous. I recognized that he was embodying the strictest interpretation of the LOA. I thought it was an interesting approach.
Apparently, though, "living as if" didn't quite work for Rob's financial
institutions. His credit card for his ad campaign with the magazine was
declined—and he left me holding a few thousand dollars in arrears.

I used the LOA for the birth of my son Dylan. I visualized having this amazing pregnancy, where I had a cute baby bump and jogged the boardwalk up until the last day of pregnancy when I would pull up to the hospital, sneeze, and out would pop the most beautiful, healthy baby. I got the healthy baby part—and that was, happily, the most important takeaway—but I need to tell you that my visualization of my cute baby bump was not achieved. Instead, I gained eighty pounds and looked similar to a rhino in heat. The sneeze was also not manifested. My labor lasted twenty-four hours, which maybe wouldn't have been so bad had I been numb from the waist down that whole time with an epidural. Unfortunately, the epidural literally fell out of my back and so the last eight hours I took a freefall from just feeling pressure and watching the contractions spike on the bedside monitor into heavy labor. In the blink of an eye, I went from bliss and excited anticipation into excruciating pain. I was so delirious with pain I was literally slamming myself in the head with a plastic bedpan. Yeah, that was most definitely *not* a sneeze! The healthy baby part, I would like to believe I manifested that, but the truth is I believe it was simply through the randomness of the Universe. I thank God for that child every day, but that randomness also brought illness into our lives and I can't believe that I was the one who manifested that.

Here's a third LOA tale. At one point, the magazine I run was failing and I began to grow weary of the process of selling ads to keep it viable. I determined a number of new ads that I needed to sell every month to stay above water. Now I visualize that I will achieve this goal each month, and that the magazine will therefore be successful. Since I began that visualization, I hit that goal each month, I get those ads. It isn't a *huge* number, it won't make me a millionaire, but the number is enough to keep the magazine going. But here is the catch—it isn't just manifestation and I don't *only* visualize that number. Yes, sometimes the sales simply just flow in, other times I chase them, but every month I hit that number. The truth is I hit that number with a combination of manifestation *and* work.

When followed too strictly, the LOA fails to account for the elbow grease I believe you need in life to make your dreams come true. This is also the thought process of the LOA detractors who say that the LOA, as it is defined, creates an apathetic approach. Stating the idea that everything in your universe is created 100 percent by your thoughts means that if someone is sick or going through a bad stretch in life, it is entirely their own fault. That is difficult for many (especially me) to swallow.

I think positive, uplifting thinking is important. I will go one step further and say it is absolutely necessary for you if you are to begin to live a more inspired life, but I believe there needs to be more. A balance of wishful thinking and hard work is what I believe in. I will call it, "LOA lite," and it espouses that like attracts like, and that you get exactly what you put out this world—not just what you wish for.

Here's simple, everyday example of LOA lite. You get on the elevator and you greet someone with a smile. Nine times out of ten, you get a smile back. That smile is often shared with someone else and so on and so on.

The Law of Attraction Lite can be summed up as a simple theory based on the elevator smile. If you smile, you will get smiles back. If you bitch and complain—and we all bitch and complain—you got it, others will join in on the bitch-fest. Don't believe me? Try it. Call your sister to bitch about your husband, and I can almost guarantee that she will bitch about hers (or worse, agree with you about yours). Two days later call her and tell her this, "I was thinking about our childhood, and it wasn't perfect but remember when we had to come to the dinner table with a current events topic? That was great." (Here is where you need to use your own memory I am pretty certain my father was the only one who mandated interesting dinner conversation from ten-year-olds. ☺) My guess is she will laugh or smile or share her own funny memory. So, yes, to all the detractors, I say like *does* attract like! But it also needs to start with a positive effort.

We all want certain things in our life and there are ways that we need to go about obtaining them. While I love the idea of manifesting, if you believe in its power alone as a means to getting what you want, you leave yourself little active control. LOA lite says manifest your dreams but don't stop with simple intention; go for it, map a plan, do the work, share the smile and then what you wish for can be yours.

So go ahead and wake up with a smile on your face (or at least smile after your first cup of coffee). Create your vision board, fill it with pictures and quotes that sum up all the goals and dreams you have. Stick it up where you will see it every day and visualize what it would be like to have those things. Then get out there and put the work in!

My belief is that when you marry manifestation with just a bit of effort, you will attract all the abundance you desire!

Reflections

VISION BOARDS ARE A FUN, CREATIVE WAY
TO SET GOALS AND INTENTIONS. YOU CAN CUT
OUT PICTURES FROM MAGAZINES, OR EVEN
SIMPLY DOODLE YOUR IDEAS. HERE IS AN EXAMPLE
OF MINE. YOU CAN FOLLOW THROUGH WITH
YOUR OWN ON THE FOLLOWING PAGE.

Vision Board

N.Y. Times
Bestselling Author
Kelly Martinsen

LBHS

Successful
Sales Rep

SHA

Reflections

IN THIS SPACE, DRAW OR SIMPLY
DOODLE PICTURES OF YOUR VISIONS,
THE THINGS YOU WANT. THIS IS A GREAT
CREATIVE EXERCISE THAT DOESN'T TAKE
MUCH TIME AND WILL REALLY HELP
YOU KEY IN TO YOUR DESIRES.

Vision Board

YOUR FEBRUARY LETTER
FROM THE PUBLISHER

March

Hello March,
I have big plans for you!

FOOD

Food: *Any nutritious substance that people or animals eat or drink, or that plants absorb, in order to maintain life and growth.*

Can you believe it is already March? It's the third month into the New Year and look at you! You are sticking to your resolution and still working on living an inspired life! *Awesome sauce!* March is a month where you can see the light. You have had enough of snow, slush, wet boots, black ice, colds, flu, stomach viruses, and shoveling. Unless you live in the Sunbelt and the only thing you have to shovel is beach sand, we are all anxiously awaiting spring's arrival. And even if you have participated and enjoyed the fun winter things like a Polar Bear Splash (You mean jumping in the ocean on New Year's Day *didn't* make your wish list? It should!), skiing in the Rockies, sledding at your neighborhood park, hot chocolate on Christmas morning, and champagne toasts on New Year's Eve, you're in a rush to see flowers growing and warm sun shining.

I do that a lot. I rush. If you recall, last month I was late for yoga class. I rushed and was totally frazzled when I got there. How often do we hear some form of the expression, "Life is the journey and not the destination"? Yet still we rush. If the winter has been particularly brutal, as was the one in which I wrote this, certainly we all see the need to rush out of it. But since we can't make time go any faster, maybe this first week of March we can simply slow down and look ahead in quiet anticipation. Rather than barreling headlong in our journey, why don't we take a moment, pause, and maybe even take a look back? Let's make March a checkpoint, a time for conscious reflection.

Perhaps you might enjoy looking *back* at your New Year's resolutions and reengaging with them. You are still moving forward on your journey in this Year of Inspired Living—and that is terrific! How are you doing with your other resolutions? Did you have the dreaded "February Fall-out"? If so, did you bounce back after a day and jump right back on that proverbial bicycle?

I failed in a few of my New Year's resolutions. One in particular that I seem to fail at a lot for some reason is the 70/30 rule that I set for myself. Fuel your body with clean food 70 percent of the time and allow yourself 30 percent wiggle room for sweets and treats (and wine ☺)! Is that one of your goals, too? If not, it should be. While we all inherently know that we must make healthier choices, you (and I) feel possessed by stress, hormones, perimenopause, menopause, thinking about menopause, or (gasp) maybe it's just plain lack of will power. Some days, I find my 70/30 ratio has literally flopped and I have spent a day eating 70 percent garbage processed food and only 30 percent good stuff.

Truth be told, as I write this I find myself sitting in my sunroom enjoying a cup of coffee partnered with a huge piece of cake—for breakfast. WTF? I have *no* excuse other than laziness (well hormones are kinda my go-to excuse, but truthfully sometimes I'm just lazy ☺). Are you like me? Here's one, food is my reward, and the thought goes like this: *Job well done, Kelly! Have some ice cream.* Even when the only job I have managed to do that day is to get my kids to school and myself to work, and then later a trip to pick up a semi-decent dinner before we all run out to sports practices for the evening. Afterwards, the kids finally head to bed—and I head to the freezer! They are all home, in bed, happy, healthy, and sleeping. *Job well done! Now pass the damn ice cream!*

The month of March is telling us something. It is telling me—specifically—to put down the ice cream and throw away my king cake (a "must buy" for a girl who lived in Alabama and enjoyed some really terrific Mardi Gras celebrations)! It is telling all of us to focus on food as *fuel*. It really is that simple. We have to constantly remind ourselves to be doctors to our own bodies, and "first do no harm." Does that seem impossible for you? Me, too! So before we both agree to give up those resolutions and just finish our breakfast of cake, cookies, and leftover pizza, let's pause. Let's look back on the promises we made ourselves on New Year's Day. Especially the resolutions we made concerning food.

I think perhaps my own relationship with food comes from childhood, when I'd get ice cream after a good report card. It also is a product of my rushing. You, too? Maybe this idea may help. When it comes time to choose a food, before you serve it or eat it, I think the key is to ask yourself the simple question: "How will this food *serve* me?" If it doesn't serve *you*, then why are you serving *it?* Be kind to yourself and recognize that you can't be 100 percent good. (Well, some people can but those folks are considerably annoying!) There are times when eating something like a piece of chocolate *will* serve you (particularly on days that you feel you might kill someone if you don't get that fix of chocolate). Perhaps our goal for March needs to be a bit more conservative: eat somewhat better than you ate the day before.

Come on, we got this, let's be present and conscious with our food choices. Throw away the word diet, and focus on lifestyle. Consciously make choices that will allow us to live the most inspired life possible. Slow . . . down . . . breathe before each bite. Write a letter to yourself and tell yourself how different you feel when you eat consciously. I will do the same. But first, I gotta finish my "breakfast" (read king cake) . . . ☺ What I can say? Rome wasn't built in a day!

Reflections

DEFINE WHAT "CONSCIOUSLY EATING" MEANS FOR YOU. DOES IT MEAN THINKING BEFORE YOU EAT OR SHOP, PUTTING THE FORK DOWN BETWEEN EACH BITE, USING A 70/30 RULE? WHATEVER IT IS, WRITE IT HERE:

TERMINATE

You cannot change the people around you,
but you can change the people you choose to be around.
—Roy T. Bennett

Terminate: *To bring to an end.*

"You're fired!"
—Donald Trump

Remember when "The Donald" was simply a host of the reality show *The Apprentice* and not the POTUS? The first time I saw the show I didn't like it. Somehow, it felt weird and intrusive watching someone's work ethic being evaluated by a boardroom full of people in Gucci suits, only to have the culminating event be a firing. I felt as if the show sent humanity back to the Dark Ages, where public hangings were the only form of entertainment. I would watch this show and say to my husband or kids, "Jeez, that's mean!" and in the very next breath say, "Wait, don't change the channel!" So I didn't like it, it didn't make me feel good, but similar to when we see a car wreck, I couldn't stop watching it.

Years ago, I worked for a biotech company. I was employed there for over thirteen years and held various jobs. One job that I held was that of district manager. In this position I was responsible for the management of ten very diverse people and the sales that they either did or didn't make for the company. I thought I was actually very well-suited for the role. I enjoyed the coaching and watching the growth and development of the sales representatives who worked for me. I truly loved sharing in their success and achievements. I can humbly but honestly tell you I was a beloved manager, and I could also say I had a team that would go to the ends of the earth for me because they saw my loyalty to them. Yet looking back, I can evaluate myself and say I may have not been the *best* manager. The only person who could answer that question would have been my own manager. I wonder now, did *my* manager think I was as effective as I could be? No, probably not.

In truth, the job of managing people takes all of the things that I listed above: nurturance, support, and loyalty. But it also takes two more things: honesty and courage. There were times when I seriously lacked both, most notably when it came to fire someone. Recognizing that the employee was not effective in the position they held and letting them go was for their benefit, for my benefit, and, ultimately, for the benefit of the company. Still, I couldn't do it. I don't think I let anyone go during my tenure as district manager, and I spent a lot of energy and focus on those people. In the end, I was lucky enough to be promoted to a different position before I had to terminate anyone (one month after my career change, three of my employees were laid off). I don't think I could have done it. I have this affliction: I genuinely love people and a bigger part of this affliction is that I want them to love me! All people! The idea of actually telling someone they "are fired" seems so cruel. But is it? Maybe not. I am older, and maybe a little bit wiser, and looking back now after my own firing, I realize that in life there comes a time where ties may need to be severed. Not just employment ties, this goes for everything, including our attachments to ideas, beliefs, and even to certain people. If you don't let go of these things, how can you make room for someone or something else.

In retrospect, I probably wasn't the best manager because I lacked a certain amount of courage. How about you? Do you find that you lack the courage it may take to remove people out of certain positions that they hold in your life?

This month was a first for me. As the publisher of *Natural Awakenings Long Island (NALI)*, I actually had to decide whether or not to "fire" an advertiser. My advertisers are *everything* to me. I want their services to be utilized because I am passionate about wellness on Long Island. Likewise, I am passionate about small businesses that offer wellness solutions through nutrition, fitness, and business coaching. I want to like and be liked by them. Who doesn't want to be liked? Forget *liking* me, more important, they *pay me!* In truth, I am their employee, I work for them. Yet in this instance, no matter how hard I worked, there was no pleasing this advertiser. In retrospect, I had probably tried too hard for too long. So, I let the client know that April would be their last contract month; I would be using the termination clause in the contract to dissolve the business relationship. Basically saying, take your money; my soul is worth more . . . or . . . "You're fired!" (Picture me as Donald Trump for full effect because that was the vision I had in my head.)

If I'd looked at this decision strictly from a business owner's point of view, it might have seemed like a wrong move since casting off this advertiser meant I lost money. Yet as a human being, I gained something more important: peace. And space. Space for another nicer, better advertising partner. When you "fire" things in your life, you ultimately make room for better things.

So how about you? Is there someone or something you should fire so that you can make room for the new? A person whose friendship has become one-sided, even toxic? A doctor who never "hears" you? Or, as in my case, you may need to fire a business associate or your boss (I say this cautiously, and in the voice of my father . . . do not quit your job until you have something else secured!). But yes, if it is time to fire the current job you are in—and doing so won't send you into a financial tailspin that will leave you more anxious and depressed than your current situation, not mention unable to afford self-help books ☺—then do it!

Sometimes it might even be a bad memory that you must fire. I once heard renowned spiritual healer Chandresh Bhardwaj say this about letting go of bad memories, "You have had your experience with the person or situation, that is your memory, but now it's time to let go. Be it an ex-lover or a beloved who has passed away, whoever it may be, release them all from your memory bank."

This month think about making room for new friends, new customers, new experiences, new jobs, new loves, and new memories by "firing" some of the less-than-positive elements in your life. Try it. You don't need a comb-over hairstyle and slightly orange skin tone for it to be effective. Look at the person, place, or thing that you are done with and, in your best Donald Trump voice, say, "Ya fiyad!" Trust me, you will be glad you did.

Reflections

MAKE PLANS: WHO OR WHAT DO YOU NEED TO FIRE FROM YOUR LIFE?

SILENCE

Silence: *Forbearance from speech or noise: muteness—
often used interjectionally.*

*The world is changed by your example,
not by your opinion.*

—Paulo Coelho

n December 2012, just two weeks before Christmas, a man (who we found out later was really just a boy) dressed in black and entered Sandy Hook Elementary School in Newtown, Connecticut, opening fire and killing multiple teachers and students. Much to America's horror, three years later, in October 2015, another man walked into a local community college, requested people stand up, and proceeded to shoot them in cold blood. Fast forward to Orlando in June 2016 to the Pulse nightclub, which catered to the LGBTQ community. A man entered the club on a busy Saturday night and began a systematic killing spree, leaving people screaming for their lives and calling their loved ones from bathrooms prior to being shot, execution style. In October 2017, a man opened fire on concert goers from his room at the Mandalay Bay hotel in Las Vegas, killing 59 people and injuring over 500 others.

If you are like me, you heard the news about these nightmares that occurred at Sandy Hook, Umpqua College, the Pulse nightclub, and the Mandalay Bay and you cried, similar to the way we all cried when we heard the news on 9/11. Evil is incomprehensible. Yet we try to understand, we try to make sense of it, and we often look for someone or something to blame (other than the killer). We also look for people to share our opinions with.

Maybe you went to Facebook or some other social media outlet after these or similar horrific events; it is a way to be with people when you can't be with people. You probably began to see posts on gun control, on politics, on mental health, on our president. People begin to argue their point of view. These tragedies become an opportunity for some to get their political points across. After incidents such as these, you often see rants about parents and their poor parenting skills, rants against guns and the NRA with counter-responses of "guns don't kill people, people kill people." I have an opinion, you have an opinion; I am sure every person watching these horrors unfold has an opinion.

I am curious as to why people use these tragedies as a soapbox platform. To literally hijack a tragedy to pontificate on your own agenda is just selfish. And in the end, isn't opinion the catalyst to most of these tragedies? Someone's opinion that America is evil, an opinion that being gay is wrong, or an opinion that the world is cruel so you should be, too—aren't these all opinions? Opinions, that when acted on, lead to devastation. Yes, opinions spoken and acted upon are selfish acts.

Selfishness is another form of evil. For humanity's sake, we can't let evil win. Evil wins if we use these horrific events and others like it to further our own agendas. Evil wins if we don't drop our opinions during these times of tragedy. Evil wins if we choose to voice our negativity, rather than sending love, prayers, and positive energy to those who are suffering. At times like these, that is what people need and not divisive opinions.

When national or world suffering is in the headlines, rather than using it as a time to pontificate and rant to further our own political agenda, how about simply praying intead. Don't pray? That's okay; then send loving thoughts to the victims. We should use tragedy to create an agenda of love, an agenda of tolerance, and then focus on how we interact with our fellow human beings.

Believe me, as an American (and publisher), I know how wonderful it is to have freedom of speech. Sometimes, though, we should remember what we learned back in nursery school, "Just because we *can* say something doesn't mean we *should*."

This letter may be a bit on the dark side. You may even be thinking, *What's the point?* This week, I think the point is there are times when we should speak less and listen more. When we listen, we learn and a small part of humanity wins. Evil wins if you begin to argue with your neighbors and friends every time a madman or a terrorist does the unspeakable and we turn it into a fight over what *we* believe caused it.

The Dalai Lama has said, "When you talk, you are only repeating what you already know. But if you listen, you may learn something new."

This week, focus a bit on practicing the art of silence. Spend less time trying to get your point across. You may discover within your silence, a sense of peace during times of chaos. Perhaps in times of tragedy you may actually need to turn away from social media and leave your opinion in its rightful place (your mind). Within your silence you can return to a focus of love: love your family, love your friends, and we can love one another. Focus your energy on love, not opinion, because if we all do that then evil loses and humanity may just win.

Reflections

WRITE YOUR OPINION ABOUT SOMETHING HERE,
AND THEN REMIND YOURSELF WHY IT IS
GOOD TO KEEP IT TO YOURSELF.

YOUR MARCH LETTER FROM THE PUBLISHER

April

"April hath put a spirit of
youth in everything."

–William Shakespeare

MEMORIAL

*No one knows how much
I cried that day.*

Memorial: *Something designed to preserve the memory of a person, event.*

y oldest sister Diana was born in April. Fifteen years ago, at age forty-five, she discovered a small spot on the back of her tongue that she thought was a canker sore. Turned out it was oral cancer.* That one spot tragically took her life. Her death feels like it just happened yesterday.

The month of April represents death and life to me. It always has. The earth is still smarting from winter, dead leaves act like mulch protecting the first blossoms of spring. Death, life.

Diana was beautiful. Fourteen years older than me, she was the epitome of the "cool older sister." She had huge dimples and long, dirty blonde hair that hung past her waist. She had a beautiful smile that literally lit up a room. She was tough, too! Anyone who knew Diana Lynn McGrath Moon understood that if you messed with her, or someone she loved, then you would surely suffer a tongue-lashing from her (oh, the irony).

Fourteen years is a *big* age difference when you are seven and your sister is twenty-one and even bigger when you are sixteen and she is in

---

* Public service announcement: April is Oral Cancer Awareness Month, so stop by your dentist for an oral cancer screening.

her thirties. She was embarking on marriage, raising kids, and owning a business while I was managing Sweet Sixteen parties, first boyfriends, and basic teenage angst. At the time we had very little in common. Aside from the age distance there was a physical distance as she was living in Texas and I in New York. There were weeks, even months, when we did not speak, living our own very different and age-appropriate lives. It is only when I reached my forties that the age gap finally became moot. Although Diana is gone, I have more in common with her now than I ever did.

It is not lost on me that I am now the exact age she was (forty-seven) when she faced the battle for her life. Sadly, she lost. There are so many things I wish I could have asked her. I'd have questions for her about raising kids and navigating the ups and downs of marriage. As a business owner, I would love to pick her brain about how she managed owning a business all those years ago. I'd especially have questions about gardening! My sister was so incredibly good at gardening, and she used to talk about it all the time. As a teenager, that was about as appealing to me as watching paint dry and I could not even make myself *pretend* to be interested in it. Yet here I am, now in my forties, and I would kill for that wisdom, that gardening conversation. At the end of Diana's life, after multiple surgeries and agonizing pain, she was left unable to speak or eat, but she could look out the window at her garden, at the earth where she planted her seeds that grew into lemon bushes, and sprawling hen-and-chickens, and roses—tons of roses. I think the garden provided her with a peaceful and beautiful respite.

When I think of April, I think of life, and of death, and of my sister Diana. I think of her beauty, and I think of her garden. Every year since her passing, I have started a garden. Within a month, my ineptness takes hold along with the weeds, reminding me that if I had my sister to call or text perhaps my garden would be successful.

I take solace in my memories. I honestly chuckle when I think about the quick wittedness of Diana's tongue; her sarcasm and honest appraisal of a situation would often leave me laughing for days. A beat down from

"D" was an awesome thing to watch and a terrible thing to be on the other end of. I miss her infectious Southern twang (which, as a born New Yorker, she always denied having ☺). I even miss hearing her call me a hated nickname: "Nelly." Yes, "Nelly" instead of "Kelly" and, yes, she based it on that bratty Nellie Oleson character from *Little House on the Prairie*. I detested when she called me that, and I threw things at her to make her stop! Right now, as I sit here writing this letter, I would kill to hear her say, "Hey NELLY!" just one more time.

While I believe in heaven, I struggle to grasp what it is exactly. I imagine it's a continuation of our energy, but maybe heaven is as simple as the memories that others use to keep us alive. They are like handprints on our hearts, which is heaven for me, and when I feel it, I am with Diana and she is with me.

I imagine we all have someone that we miss so much it hurts. I think it's good to embrace that pain, not to cut it off or stifle it. Your loss is only painful because of the loving relationship you once shared. Stifling that pain would only stifle the amazing memories that are like a slice of heaven. I believe that those whom we have "lost" are really not lost, if there is a place you can go to find them.

For me, it is my garden. Every April I head out, I prepare my soil, and I plant. Even if I end up with a mess of weeds by August, come the next April you can once again find me eagerly sowing, planting, and tilling. It took me about ten years to figure out that I am not planting with the goal of a bountiful harvest (although that would be great). No, I am planting in my garden because it is my piece of heaven, and when I am out there digging in the soil, it is with the hope that I hear Diana's voice just one more time. Even if it is only in my mind, and even if it is only to hear her say, "Really Nelly? You call *that* a garden?" ☺

Reflections

WHOM DO YOU MISS? CAN YOU SEE THEM?
CAN YOU HEAR THEM? SIMPLY WRITE DOWN HOW
BLESSED YOU ARE TO FEEL THAT HANDPRINT
FOREVER ON YOUR HEART. REMIND YOURSELF
WHERE YOU CAN FIND THAT ESSENCE
OF CLOSENESS, THEN GO THERE.

INDIFFERENCE

The opposite of love is not hate, it's indifference. The opposite of beauty is not ugliness, it's indifference. The opposite of faith is not heresy, it's indifference. And the opposite of life is not death, but indifference between life and death.
— Elie Wiesel

Indifference: *Lack of interest or concern.*

The other day, I went for a run. I ran down a street just two blocks from the ocean. Beautiful, right? The sound of the waves, the smell of the ocean—then *bam*, squish, I stepped right into a pile of dog crap. As I looked down, I noticed not one but multiple piles of (sh)it scattered over the sidewalk adjacent to a crappy—in more than one way—lawn. You can tell a lot about a person by the way he or she treats the earth.

I had four more miles to run, giving me ample time to reflect on the people who don't clean up after their dogs. I live in a nice town, not wealthy but nice, and so close to the ocean that the real estate isn't cheap. So the people who live here pay a fair amount of money for that location, and I would imagine if they chose to live in this town they probably *love* the ocean. Don't they know that their dog's waste will eventually be washed by the rain into the storm drains, which eventually lead to the ocean that they more than likely love to swim in? That their dog's crap will end up in the seafood that they, their friends, and family might eat?

Do they *want* to eat and swim in their dog's feces? I wondered about all of this as I ran. I've got to believe they don't! Yet, either they *do* want to eat and swim in their dog's poo, or they are ignorant and don't recognize the consequences—or a worse possibility is that they know and yet they are indifferent to it. They literally don't give a sh*t (or pick up a sh*t). They don't care enough to bend down and clean it up! I believe indifference breeds the worst kind of danger to mankind.

With a mile or two left to run, I got to thinking about the subject of indifference. I had recently seen the movie *The Hunger Games* with my children. If you haven't seen it, it's a science fiction movie where kids are chosen by lottery to fight to the death as a televised, publicized sport. Science fiction, right? Yes, absolutely, which is why it made sense when my daughter said, "It was a good movie but hard to believe because in real life, I mean come on, Mom, people would not treat each other the way they did in that movie." Out of the mouth of babes! You can imagine my daughter's surprise not two days later when my family watched the Oscar-winning movie *12 Years a Slave*. Based on a true story, it illustrated to her just how horribly humans actually can treat one another and how indifferent we can be to another's plight, especially if it makes our own life easier.

You can easily detach yourself from compassion, empathy, and humanity if doing so offers you a less difficult existence. It starts with something as simple as not picking up dog crap because you bending down far too difficult. So that poop eventually gets into our waterways. *Jeez, it's just dog poop!* you may be thinking, but I say it illustrates something bigger; it illustrates indifference. History has shown that indifference can perpetrate much higher costs.

Indifference is the reason videos go viral, including the video of a fourteen-year-old actor, freezing and without a coat on a brutal winter day, begging for money as people walked past not even looking his way—that is until a *real* homeless person came up to him and gave him his coat. Haven't seen it? In the video clip[3], you can hear the homeless man saying, "It's tough out here and we need to look out and take care

3. *https://www.youtube.com/watch?v=5CwCvpEMEJU*

of one another." Yes, yes, yes, we do need to look out for one another; we need to break free from our chains of indifference.

Indifference is something that is learned from one generation to another. If you have children it is even more important that you demonstrate love, kindness, caring, and empathy. This world, this ecosystem that God created and that we live in, is built specifically to show the value of every single creature.

Okay, so now the task before you. Yes, you will try not to be indifferent . . . *How in the hell do you do* that? you may be thinking. I believe it starts with being aware, moving your thoughts from "me" to "we," and then it takes action. Stop and give a dollar to the person on the street (more if you've got it). Find an organization you can get behind and volunteer! There is nothing more fulfilling then volunteer work. Even the simple act of meeting a friend for lunch is moving one step further away from indifference. Seriously, the simple act of taking a phone call from your relative or friend when you are sure you don't have a minute to spare for them helps to erase indifference. If you see an injustice, have the courage to do something about it.

There are a million other ways to prevent indifference. Perhaps it can be as easy as remembering to recycle. You may say, "I don't litter, I already recycle, I got this," but I would state that it is taking that *one step further* that keeps you from being indifferent. For instance, when you see trash on the street, rather than walking past it thinking, *What pig left that here?* pick that trash up. When you encounter someone who looks like they are in need, make eye contact and smile at them. That smile could be the thing that stops them from going home and ending their life. It's called the butterfly effect and it is a theory that the flap of butterfly's wings on one side of the world could literally cause a hurricane thousands of miles away. Dropping indifferent tendencies can have that sort of wide-ranging impact on our planet and on humanity. Be a beautiful butterfly and cause a hurricane of kindness. Flap your wings, relieve yourself of your indifferent nature, and—not to sound too cliché, but I will say it—go ahead, "Be the change . . . "

Reflections

HOW CAN YOU BREAK THE CYCLE
OF INDIFFERENCE IN YOUR COMMUNITY?

TOMORROW

What if you woke up tomorrow with only the things you thanked God for today?

Tomorrow: *A mystical day where 99 percent of all human productivity, motivation, and achievement is stored.*

"Tomorrow" is such a beautiful word! Tomorrow offers you opportunity and another chance to figure out your God-given purpose in this world (yes, you have one, maybe even more than one). Tomorrow offers you forgiveness, too. Like when you start a diet, eating clean all week and feeling great, and then reward yourself with beer and loaded nachos on the weekend. That can't be just me! We can tell ourselves, *I'll get back to it tomorrow.* (Thank goodness because, honestly, it was a long week and I *really needed* that beer and nachos!) It happens with fitness as well (does it ever! ☺). One day, we run optimally, then the next day we're unable to finish a mile without taking a break to walk. Or when our yoga poses feel perfect one day—strong, beautiful even—and then the next day our "warrior one" pose looks and feels more like it should be called "wounded warrior." How about at work? I am sure we have all experienced that workday or workweek where we are riding along on a wave of success, only to watch as someone else gets the promotion, the raise, the accolades. Or worse, we make a silly mistake on the job and come tumbling off that wave of success.

Currently, I am working on a book (I must have finally finished it if you are in fact reading it). But it took much longer than it should have. I would start writing, only to see an email pop up or a photo on Facebook that *needed* my "like" or "comment" distracting me so much I wouldn't even remember where I was going with my prose.

Wait, where was I? ☺ Oh, yes, tomorrow . . . There is always tomorrow. Until there isn't. Because, reality tells us, our tomorrows here on Earth are limited.

What does tomorrow offer to you? I think the answer is ridiculously simple. It offers you: One. More. Day. Isn't that the goal? The pursuit of having one more day. Isn't that the reason you eat healthy and exercise? Because of a belief that it will equate to longevity? Tomorrow offers hope, opportunity, blessings, random encounters, and the time to forgive. One day more offers the opportunity to make up from that argument; to get over the anger felt about a perceived injustice; to take out your cookbook and get back on the road to eating healthfully; to get on your spin bike or hop up into a headstand (yes, I know, any yogi worth her salt does not *hop* into a headstand); another day to kiss your loved ones; and one more day offers you a chance to make a stranger smile. Perhaps most important, tomorrow gives you another day to forgive yourself for yesterday's failures. One more day provides space and time—a well-needed distance from the prior day's events that might provide some clarity. No matter how bad it seems today, and for some of you reading this it may seem really, *really* bad, tomorrow provides the precise calculation of distance and time that you may need to change your perception and to allow random engagements with others that may simply change your life's trajectory. When it seems it absolutely can't get any worse, and then you wake up and tomorrow hands you even worse . . . there is still always another tomorrow with blessings waiting to be had.

Tomorrow. The place where 99 percent of all your achievement is stored! Tomorrow is on its way, and with it, endless possibility.

Reflections

PUT IN WRITING WHAT YOU HATED ABOUT TODAY. BEFORE YOU GO TO SLEEP CROSS IT ALL OUT!

YOUR APRIL LETTER
FROM THE PUBLISHER

May

Hello, May.
Surprise me.

MOTHER

I love the mothers teaching their toddlers Japanese while I'm over here just trying to get mine to stop licking the refrigerator.

Mother: *Not a person to lean on but a person who makes leaning unnecessary, as defined by Dorothy Fisher.*

I have held a job since I was fourteen years old and my father forged working papers for me. In the '80s, I scooped ice cream at Friendly's restaurant and sold tablecloths at Fortunoff department store. In the '90s, I was the woman on the phone in the morning calling you to ask for your donation to your alma mater and serving you a beer and fries at the local college bar in the evening. Those were tough jobs, however, my work these days is much harder. I don't like to complain, but my work environment is often hostile, and I have been met with disrespect and have even been told, "I hate you." My work is so intense that it can rip apart my soul at times—just like lightning through a cloud—and then just as quickly as the storm comes, it passes and I'm met with a rainbow of love and gratitude from the people I work for. Seriously, my work environment is bipolar at best and psychotic at its worst. I don't want to sound self-important, but in my job it is absolutely critical that I handle matters both delicately and firmly. I try to explain to my "bosses" (I have two) over and over that while I *want* to do everything for them, I

71

simply can't do *everything* for them. They don't understand that while I would gladly be their "bridge" over each and every one of their troubles, it requires much more courage not to do so.

I am not speaking about my job as publisher of *Natural Awakenings* magazine. No, my real job—the one that keeps me up at night—is the job of being a parent.

Have you seen the "World's Toughest Job Interview" on YouTube? It's a brilliant ad for Hallmark and is a video of a man interviewing multiple people for an operations manager job. An ad agency posted a classified ad for the "job," then conducted interviews via Skype and recorded the candidates' reactions to some truly inane job requirements.

"If you had a life, we'd ask you to . . . sort of give that life up," the interviewer tells applicants. "No vacations. In fact, on Thanksgiving, Christmas, New Year's—all holidays—the workload is going to go up, and we demand that."

The interviewer continues with a litany of requirements, including:

- You are required to work standing up most or all of the time.
- You work twenty-four hours a day, no breaks.
- It would be excellent if you held a degree in medicine, finance, *and* culinary arts.
- You may need to stay up with your client throughout the night, and then comes the kicker . . .
- Oh, and no pay!

Reaction from the interviewees is priceless: "Is that even legal?" said one millennial. "That sounds twisted," said another, "inhumane."

The end of the video reveals this is really the job description for a twenty-first century mother. The mother who sacrifices her own needs and desires (and in my own case, often my sanity), juggling the demands of family in the role of mother. The mother who feels it is a badge of honor to give of herself until she breaks. The mother who, thanks to Google, knows the answers to all problems including, but not limited to, getting rid of lice, eating disorders, bullying, and ear infections. We mothers know everything. We give these kids everything. They are our everything, and perhaps subconsciously we want to be their everything.

This job is made even harder for some if they have a proclivity toward being a control freak like me. Allowing our children to fall, fight, fail, and feel pain is so much harder than just fixing every problem for them. Teaching our children to "build their own bridge" often feels cruel. Fueled by our never-ending love for them, we want to save them from their first broken heart. We want protect them from the meanness of other children and at the same time to protect our children from their own capacity for meanness; knowing that both can lead to pain and, even worse, regret.

Personally, I am blinded by my desire for my children's unending happiness. But that isn't real, is it? Unending happiness? Of course not. They must know the feeling of that very first heartbreak so that they know they can overcome it. They must experience a sports or academic failure (without a nosy parent calling the coach or teacher) so that they feel the desire to do better the next time.

In spite of our need to protect them from unpleasantness, they must experience disappointment, face pain, and, ultimately, build bridges so that they truly experience the opposite—success and happiness. I believe that my children are aware that their parents root for their success and love them unconditionally. And while I watch them navigate through life, I am comforted that my children know that if they were to get to a place where all seems absolutely lost, that I would move heaven and earth to save them. I hope that with that knowledge in their hearts, perhaps I may never have to.

The month of May is special because it has a day within it that is exclusively for honoring mothers. Can women be successful mothers and at the same time have their own success? I believe the answer is not only yes we can but also yes we *must*! I witnessed it firsthand with my own mother. In the 1970s, she began as a stay-at-home mom and yet managed to assist with my father's company, play tennis, have three date nights a week (yes, always with my father), and she even vacationed at least twice a year without her children ☺ (gasp). I didn't realize it then, but she was balancing her roles. My mother had her own personal successes. She had her own friends (not friends she made because of the kids) and, honestly, her own beautiful life. I was lucky enough to be part of her universe but luckier still because I was not the *center* of that universe! As a child, I never doubted she loved me and that she would go to the ends of the earth for me, but she was not easily manipulated, and didn't hover like the "helicopter parents" we see so much of today.

My mother stressed independence, stronger than any other parent I have come into contact with until this day. Don't believe me? Here's an example: I attended sleep-away camp three states away, at the age of just six years old. Yup, at this young and tender age, I boarded a Greyhound bus leaving from the Port Authority Station in Times Square (yes, 1970's Times Square!) and rode it to Massachusetts with about ten other children ages nine to sixteen. We didn't have any chaperones, though the camp did tell Greyhound that we were minors traveling alone. It wasn't even a direct bus, we actually had to transfer to a second bus once in the city of Hartford, Connecticut, and that bus would take us into Boston, Massachusetts, where a camp van would pick us up and take us to what would be our home for the next few weeks.

Looking back on this as an adult, it is almost funny, a running family joke told every holiday. Whenever the topic of my time at camp comes up, the conversation goes something like this:

- Mom: "Oh Kelly, you are exaggerating. I don't think you were six!"
- Kelly: "Oh yes, Mom, I was."
- Mom: "Well you enjoyed camp didn't you?"

She's right, I loved it, but no matter how much fun I had, I am 100 percent sure I would not have the balls to send my own kindergartener on the same adventure (which may be unfortunate for her). If you think my mother was detached, you are wrong. She was "there" so consistently that when I exited my tumultuous teens and successful twenties and it was time to pick my maid of honor for my wedding, she was my first choice. My mom is amazing. The perfect role model, happily engaging in her life and letting me be a part of it. She is a rock who faced terrible pain in her life, including the loss of not one but two daughters. She was an angel in her unwillingness to burden her remaining children with that pain. I am blessed and thankful every day for the way she raised me! To this day, I wish I had the courage to raise my own children in much the same way. I don't but I wish I did.

Mothers are not only the women who birth us. "Mothers" are often the women who come into our lives unexpectedly. They are our teachers, mentors, coaches, and even in-laws! (Yup, I said it, IN-LAWS!) Imagine my shock when I won the "mother lottery" a second time around after marrying my husband. Everyone loves my mother-in-law (me included!). If you are reading this book, there is a nine out of ten chance that she gave you your copy! She champions her children's successes. She travels around the country to see her grandchildren's lacrosse games. She is warm and nurturing, and when we first got married sometimes I even liked to say, "Let's go sleep at your parents' house tonight." I knew we'd wake to a wonderful hot breakfast. Yet with all this natural "mothering ability" she, too, has always had her *own* life. She was vice president of a bank in the 1980s, a career woman before that was in vogue! She loved her children and she doted on them and punished them when necessary (my husband was one that often needed a lot of punishing!), but she had her *own* life.

This was a rather long prose telling you about two amazing women and mothers, Marilyn McGrath and Elizabeth Martinsen. Why? Because they are uniquely different in their approach to womanhood and to motherhood, but they both insisted on living a rewarding life that was not centered on their children. Do you resemble them as women and mothers? Or are you honestly a bit more like me? So in love with these little creations (sometimes I call them creations, sometimes monsters) that you have brought into the world that you don't want them to cry for even one minute. Do you hover over your child's cell phone just to see if everyone is being nice? Do you contact your daughter's school to tell the principal that your son or daughter is getting too much homework, or not enough homework . . . that one is *always* my favorite . . . you know *that* mom (please tell me *you* are not *that* mom). Are your children older now and do you find your Saturday nights are spent similar to that of an Uber driver, waiting to see where your next text will take you? Have your children left the nest? If so, do you find yourself slightly lacking the purpose that you had when they were home?

You may be reading this thinking, *You're right, it's not fair to me to have given up my dreams and pursuits simply to help my children live their life*. I will go one step further and tell you that it also isn't fair to your children. It is too much pressure for them to be responsible for your every smile. They are happier when they see us working, or volunteering, or doing anything that takes the focus off them. We need to model self-sufficient, self-loving behavior. Sometimes, all it takes to do this is a simple "yes." When your spouse says, "Let's go away, just the two of us," answer, "Yes." When your friend says, "Let's go to dinner," answer, "Yes." When a co-worker says, "Let's try a new sport, enter a running race, take a hula-hoop class, find a tribe (a group of women you connect with)," answer, "YES!" *Yes* to yourself, *yes* to discovering what you can do at any age, and *yes* to keeping your children in your universe without actually rotating around them!

Reflections

WHAT ACTIVITY CAN YOU ADD TO YOUR LIFE THAT IS JUST FOR YOU AND NOT FOCUSED ON SOMEONE ELSE?

PATIENCE

Patience: *The capacity to accept or tolerate delay, trouble, or suffering without getting angry or upset.*

O h my goodness, my friend makes me crazy. Seriously, she drives me nuts. She is happy one minute and miserable the next. When I call her, I don't know which person is going to pick up the phone! (So I don't, call her that is. Not often.)

Oh my goodness, I have to be at work by 9 a.m. but my kids are leisurely crunching their cereal—and with an open mouth! I may strangle them.

Oh my goodness, I have been dieting for three weeks straight, and I've only lost three pounds. WTF?

It is evident as we age, our ability to institute patience into our lives becomes less and less likely. Not sure why, maybe it is hormones or previous life experiences, but whatever the reason, lately everything (including my own personality!) is getting on my nerves.

How are you with patience? Does it come to you readily? Or are you like me, taking large exaggerated breaths, grinding your teeth, or, worse, are you slowly losing your shit as you scream, "HURRY UP WE GOTTA GET TO SCHOOOOOOOOOOOOOOL!" at a pitch so high it may break glass.

If you are patient, all the time, with the needy friend or co-worker, the aging parents, the kids, the husband, and the asshole who cut you off on the road today, well then skip this. Seriously, don't let me bring you into an impatient zone.

Still with me? I thought so. So let's get at it. Patience. I was thinking so much about the word I almost lost mine. What keeps coming back to me is "kindness." I thought, *Kelly, change this and make this letter focus on kindness, seriously, who are you kidding? How can you talk about patience?* It hit me that patience is a form of kindness. *Kindness, the quality of being friendly, generous, and considerate.* If we are friendly, generous, and considerate, then how can we be impatient? We gain patience by having these three attributes.

Friendly. That's the act of being a friend, even to the most annoying and needy of friends. Generous. Well, be generous with people, with your time, and with your energy, with your kind words, and with your smile. Considerate. The time that it takes to consider another person's feelings or life situation is critical to being able to offer someone patience.

I have a friend who is elderly, close to ninety years old. He is a family friend and I see him at family celebrations. He had been sick and I hadn't seen him in a while. At a family gathering recently, I saw him sitting alone on the couch watching a hockey game. "Hey, where's Kevin?" he asked.

"He is skiing out west in Lake Tahoe with my son Dylan," was my reply.

He proceeded to tell me a bit about his time in California, and how great it was—until his wife showed up. He chuckled, "That's when all the fun stopped!" We laughed, then there was silence, and he looked up and said, "Hey, where's Kevin?" My heart stopped. I had recently heard he had been suffering from early Alzheimer's but had no idea how bad it had gotten. I didn't know what to do, I mean I just told him "Lake Tahoe." Would he remember once I said it again? Would he feel embarrassed? Honestly, would I hear the exact same story ending with, "that's when the fun stopped"? I am being honest and I am not proud of this, but my first wish was that someone would come over and sit with us and I could get out of this uncomfortable situation. No one was in the vicinity, so instead of "Lake Tahoe" I said, "He is out West," thinking maybe it would trigger a different memory.

He spoke about his time out West (again) and ended with laughter and, "That's when the fun stopped!" We both looked at the game. I could have gotten up then, someone else was in the vicinity that I had wanted to speak to about something, but instead I sat with him in what for me was an uncomfortable silence. He turned toward me and asked, "Hey, where's Kevin?" We spent about twenty minutes having the same conversation while my heart was slowly breaking for him, for his children, and for the realization that there is absolutely no reason that I should not be this patient with every single person I meet—including myself.

There are times, whether it's when we are dealing with toddlers or dealing with the elderly, that require a lot of patience. That makes sense. Running late? A paper or project due for work? Someone cuts you off or you cheat on your diet for the billionth time? In those situations, an impatient reaction just doesn't make sense, it's too extreme, it's wasted energy, it's . . . silly.

Exhibiting patience is a kindness. Patience with our friends, our children, our spouse, strangers, and, yes, patience with our own imperfections.

This letter and the actions requested of you are incredibly difficult. Trust me, I have been trying to exhibit more patience this entire week and it was hard. It was only when I switched that word in my head from "patience" to "kindness" that my task became more doable. And honestly it is doable. Be just a little bit kinder than is your norm. It will bring you a bit of calm, too. You will discover, like I did, that when you offer someone else the kindness of patience, you suck the crazy right out of a situation. The difficult or chaotic feeling that could envelop you is replaced with a calm feeling and, dare I say, when you offer that kindness and the gift of patience you also feel proud of yourself. You trust that you are being *exactly* who you want to be. You are "publishing" the authentic self that you want the world to see. So let's refrain from yelling when our kids are late, or a guy cuts us off on the road (I use this one a lot; perhaps the next book should be a self-help road-rage book ☺), or when work deadlines have us crawling out of our skin. And yes, answer repeat questions as often as you can because life is short and unpredictable, and you never know when you will hear for the last time, "Hey, where's Kevin?" ☺

SHINE

Don't ever let anyone
dull your sparkle.

Shine: *To give out a bright light.*

Who Am I to Be Brilliant?
"Our deepest fear is not that we are inadequate.
Our deepest fear is that we are powerful beyond measure.
It is our light, not our darkness, that most frightens
us. We ask ourselves, Who am I to be brilliant,
gorgeous, talented, fabulous? Actually, who are you
not to be? You are a child of God. Your playing small
does not serve the world. There is nothing enlightened
about shrinking so that other people won't feel
insecure around you. We are all meant to shine,
as children do… And as we let our own
light shine, we unconsciously give other people
permission to do the same."
—Marianne Williamson

*T*he other day I had my hair cut. You got it! My hair looked *gooooooood!* I had taken a day off to run some errands, one of which was to finally dye my hair (a little vainglory never hurt anyone), and I also bought a new top. I felt great as I went to pick up my kids from school. I ran into my friend Christine who said, "You look so pretty!" Someone thought I looked great: mission accomplished. But then more moms came around, and while they were all beautifully kind in their compliments, there were some questions thrown in. "What's the occasion?" "Are you going somewhere?" I wasn't insulted, exactly, these women were being nice; so why didn't I feel comfortable? I think it was because *they* didn't feel comfortable. They joked about their sweats and their yoga pants. Then I reached for my old standard, self-effacing humor to put them at ease, "Oh you know me, ladies. While I rock my 'homeless look' most of the time, I have a work event tonight and that's why I look like this." Working from home every day as a writer/publisher, I usually wear stained sweatpants and my husband's old flannel shirt, so my self-effacing "homeless look" comment was true, but my remark about having a "work thing" was absolutely not. My hair blown out and new outfit made them uncomfortable, which then made me uncomfortable, so I hid behind self-deprecating humor and a little white lie.

Why does it make others feel uncomfortable when someone changes up the silently agreed-upon rule of "you and I, we wear sweats"? Most of the time, I have to admit, this is an awesome rule. But when we break it, do we really need to hear, "Why are you so dressed up?" As women we need to stop asking each other that question. We don't need a reason to shine. We don't need an excuse to throw on a beautiful dress, great shoes, or even, in my case, sometimes just a dab of blush.

What I should have said was, "Yeah I had a great day, I got things done just for me and the hair is one of those things." By saying that, I would have given unwritten approval for these other women to do the same!

How about sharing your talents? Some are easier to share than others. I have two friends who both have amazing voices. First, there's my friend who I'll call Beth. I know about her beautiful voice because I overheard her singing once in college, while she was cooking dinner. I asked her, "Do you sing anywhere else, a club, a church?"

She smiled and said, "Yeah, sometimes I sing in the shower."

The other friend—I will call her Olivia—is a new friend. We are "Facebook friends," which is fun! Once in a while she puts up a video of herself singing. She shines! Listening to her God-given talent makes me smile. I also admire her guts for putting it out there for people to judge.

Are you friend Beth or are you friend Olivia? I bet 90 percent of people reading this are Beth. You are someone who hides their light. Don't wait for a major opportunity or worse, a crisis, to show you are brilliant, talented, and wise beyond what anyone sees. Live your life shining. Every day, be the same gorgeous "selfie" that you post (or the selfie that you take and don't post).

The truth is that everything has a domino effect. If you shine, you give someone else permission to shine. It is compounding. When I see my friend singing on Facebook, it makes me happy and proud of her light. It makes me think, *I can't sing* (I am able to, but trust me, you would *not* want to hear it!), *but I can stand-up paddle surf in head-high waves; maybe I should share that.* When I do, I believe I subconsciously give others that same permission that Olivia gave me—permission to shine!

We need to let go of crippling thoughts about what the "haters" may think, and focus on the fact that if we shine, if we share our brilliance, others will do the same. Could you imagine a world in which everyone—and I mean everyone—caught the contagious virus called "shining"? What a bright and beautiful world that would be. The guitar you want to play, the screenplay in your computer that you want to finish, the coaching you want to be involved in, the garden you want to start, the modeling you want to do, the art you want to bring to the world, the joke you want to tell, or the story you want to share—do it! Share it with the world! Shine. Shine. Shine. What are you waiting for? When you do allow yourself to shine, the universe will react in return with even more awesomeness from other women (and men). You can then bask in the glory of what you started. Because deep down you must know that "playing small does *not* serve the world." The truth is that perhaps the woman next to you on the train, or the friend that you have coffee with, or sit with at PTA meetings, is simply waiting for you to show your light before she is able to show hers. Come on, help her out, dress up to leave the house, even if it is just to go get eggs, sing publically, share your hidden talents . . . SHINE, and watch the domino effect.

Reflections

WHAT ARE YOU GOOD AT THAT YOU CAN SHARE WITH THE WORLD?

YOUR MAY LETTER
FROM THE PUBLISHER

June

"And since all this
loveliness can not be Heaven,
I know in my heart it is June."

—Abba Gould Woolson

FILIAL PIETY

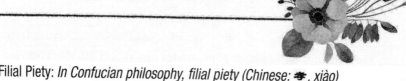

I never know what to give my father for Christmas.
I gave him $100 and said, "Buy yourself
something that will make your life easier."
So he went out and bought a present for my mother.

—Rita Rudner

Filial Piety: *In Confucian philosophy, filial piety (Chinese: 孝, xiào) is a virtue of respect for one's parents, elders, and ancestors.*

Dan Fogelberg has long been one of my favorite singer-songwriters. When I hear his music now, I am reminded of the 1970s, and the easy life of a ten-year-old. I think about my parents, my father mostly. Specifically, Fogelberg's song "Leader of the Band." Not familiar with it? It's beautiful and the lyrics poignant, so when you finish this chapter find it on Spotify (or Pandora or wherever ☺). In it, he thanks his father, who was a musician and bandleader, for a few things: the music, his stories, freedom, kindness, and even for the times when "he got tough." The most poignant part of the song for me, though, is when he sings that he didn't say "I love you" near enough.

My relationship with my father is anything but perfect—you show me a forty-seven-year relationship that is! Yet, every time I hear the Dan Fogelberg song "Leader of the Band," it makes me think of my dad. It sums up, in my view, what my father offered to my sisters and me as we grew up on Long Island.

MUSIC. When I was younger, and even now, my father shared with me his love of music. As such, you can hear me belting Broadway show tunes on any given Sunday during my four-mile run. Dad shared, without saying a word, that music can turn a bad mood good and can make the most boring of events (cleaning my room) somewhat tolerable. Through his music, he shared growing up in Queens, New York, during the Depression; living through World War II; his first job; his first major life decisions, such as joining the Air Force and the ROTC ("They were offering a free pair of shoes to anyone who joined, Kelly! Of course I would sign up!"); his first date with my mom; his decision to start his own company; and more. All of it was highlighted in the music that would be playing through our home.

STORIES. Here's one. My grandfather didn't think his son, my father, had what it took to obtain good grades in a rigid Catholic school setting. When my father came to him stating that he intended to take the Catholic School Entrance Exam, my grandfather said he would not pay for it because my dad lacked "grades and work ethic." My father got into two schools, Chaminade on Long Island and The Most Holy Trinity (TMHT) in Queens. While he desperately wanted to attend Chaminade, neither he nor his father could afford the tuition, but TMHT was only $50. He went to his father who again refused to pay his tuition and again recommended that he attend the local public school in Hollis, Queens. My father got a job that summer (in truth, he *always* had some job), he saved his money, and at the end of the summer he paid the $50 from his earnings and attended TMHT. When his report card arrived showing how well he had done, my grandfather, a rather removed man, handed him $50 and said, "I guess I was wrong." My grandfather never discussed it again, never said a word, yet he paid for his schooling for the next four years. Reflecting on the story, my father, a rather stoic man himself, began to tear up. That surprised him (and shocked the hell out of me), and then he laughed at himself and said, "I didn't think it was that special at the time; I am not sure why I am reacting like this now after all these years."

FREEDOM: Well, if you read this book with any consistency, you're aware that my parents offered me freedom. Like the freedom to hop a Greyhound bus headed for a Massachusetts sleep-away camp at age six. But they also supported me with the freedom to pursue an acting career and live in New York City after finishing college. This freedom was made available to me even when freedom may have been the last thing in the world they wanted to give me. As a disclaimer, I should state that I was not so free that I wasn't immediately punished if I broke my 10:30 p.m. curfew (a full hour earlier than that of my friends). But I did have freedom. Freedom also to make mistakes. So I journeyed, and I tried things and I failed and I succeeded. I am sure watching that was tough at times for my parents.

KINDNESS. As a parent myself now, I get how that freedom-kindness fulcrum works. Yes, you need to offer your children freedom; yes, they will make mistakes; yes, your act of kindness will be offering them forgiveness and, even more than that, understanding. Understanding that a teenager's frontal lobe isn't even fully developed (seriously they know not what they do) and kindness when they are hurting. The toughest time to be kind is when your children are not being kind to you. Recognize with kindness that the act of yelling and screaming at you is often just a test, a test to see if they can break a bit away from you without breaking into pieces. Don't have a teen yet? Trust me, they will be unkind; answer it with kindness.

TIME TO GET TOUGH. All dads should be kind—that is until they need to get tough. My own teenage years were turbulent, so I saw my father's tough side a lot during that period. Thank God! I do not want to think where I would be now had he not been tough, very tough. As a teenager, I am positive I would have made poor choices when given the above-mentioned freedom had there not been limits on my life. My father was never afraid of punishing me. He was never afraid of losing my love and admiration. He didn't waver. He punished and he walked away. Because of this unwavering toughness, I never tried to manipulate a situation with tears. I knew it wouldn't work. There are times when we absolutely must be tough. When we cross that line to the tough side, the most important part of my father's toughness was that he didn't falter. He never went back and let us out of a punishment. There were a few days, sometimes a few weeks, of lost liberties and then I was let out . . . to see what I would do next. If I failed in using my freedom wisely, again I would be punished, I would lose those freedoms. This consistency was a blessing.

The most important part of this letter, for me, is the last part. Dan Fogelberg wrote this song as his father was dying, and it is poignant that at the very end he recognizes that he didn't tell his father he loved him nearly enough. Do we ever? Lord, I try. This is true in every relationship, not just those with our parents or children. I wonder why that is? Why we don't say I love you more often?

I think Dan Fogelberg gives us some amazing advice to use in any relationship and I have seen firsthand how successful it can be. The five ideas held within this song absolutely work in any and every relationship. Share your music and your stories. Offer freedom and kindness. When necessary, have the guts to get tough. And never, ever believe for one moment that you have said, "I love you" near enough.

Reflections

HOW WILL YOU SHARE YOUR MUSIC, STORIES, FREEDOM, AND KINDNESS WITH THOSE YOU LOVE?*

Exercise suggestion for a Saturday or Sunday afternoon: take your headphones off and go song-for-song with your kids on your house speaker. Play one of your songs, then one of theirs. No rules, no judgment. (Trust me, when you hear the crap they listen to you will want to judge. Don't!)

INSPIRATION

To be inspired is great, to inspire is incredible.

Inspiration: *A divine influence or action on a person believed to qualify him or her to receive and communicate sacred revelation.*

There was a recent *Natural Awakenings* publishers' conference in Florida, which was said to have been amazing. I wasn't able to attend, so I asked my friend—another publisher—who was there what it was that made the experience so great and what knowledge she gleaned from it. I was looking for publishing insight, so you can imagine my surprise when she laughed and said, "It was transformative, and when I left I knew I had to get new friends—that the friends I have actually suck!" I laughed with her, secretly hoping I wasn't one of those "sucky friends." She continued, "I realize that these women that I play tennis and golf with at my club (*whew*, I am neither), they are not *real* and that I'm not interested in continuing in uninspiring relationships." Good for her! I look forward to hearing about her journey making new friends in her fifties—friends that inspire her.

How about you? Do the people you surround yourself with *inspire* you? For me the answer is, yes!

I have had the incredible opportunity to witness a coach of a local wrestling team, Miguel Rodriquez, who inspires me daily. At this point, if you need a break from this book or feel like surfing the net, hop on your computer and search for an ESPN piece called "Isaiah Bird No Excuses." When you do, you will be floored at the *abilities* that this young man possesses. A second-grade student at the time of the initial airing, Isaiah is a little boy who has no legs. In his lifetime he has suffered other complications, including financial and family struggles. But those "problems" are not what you will see on the video, you will see something deeper. You will witness and be inspired by this young boy doing the most with what he has. You will also see my friend, a local teacher's assistant and wrestling coach, who becomes a "father" to young Isaiah. In the video, Coach says, "I am like a dad. I know I am not his dad." No words have ever impacted me as much as those have. Cue tears, beautiful story, and if it ended right there you would be moved, you would be inspired. Except it doesn't end right there for Miguel Rodriguez.

We are part of the Long Beach wrestling community that calls itself "La Familia." The father of that team of boys is Rodriguez, aka "Papi." Many of our young wrestlers live extremely tough lives, living in Section 8 public housing with no parents, or parents who are so overworked that a young male can easily be forgotten or easily wind up with the wrong influences. The other boys may have too much: beautiful homes on the shores of Long Beach, fancy cars, and more, and they may get into a little trouble with their excess. Not on Rodriguez's watch. He is on these boys', every move. He calls them to locate them, he yells at them when they go astray, and he praises them when they work hard. He is father/big brother to every single one of these boys. He recognizes their poverty, or lack of parental guidance, or even their entitled excess, but he does not for one second allow them to utilize it as an excuse or a crutch. He pushes, he expects, and he loves each and every one of them. He is "their dad" who knows he is "not their dad." I am blessed to have him in my life as a daily reminder of how we as human beings can inspire one another.

This chapter could be done here. With me asking you to surround yourself with the Miguel Rodriguez's of the world. But it won't. Because I think they may be a bit hard to find in the current climate. So instead I task you not to simply surround yourself with inspirational people, but instead for *you* to become inspirational. *Wait what?* you may be thinking, *Honestly, I just wanted to read a book and maybe journal a bit and now you are asking me to be inspiring?* Yes I am. Because you can be!

Oh, I don't expect you to start fathering or mothering young people (unless you feel you can). I am simply saying that we can all—including myself, always—do more to be of service to others. We can start by choosing to surround ourselves with the people who make us want to do more and to be more. To connect to people who inspire us and thus motivate us to live a more engaged life of service.

But then *we* must get to the service part. There are multiple opportunities to live a life of service. You can run a race for a good cause; you can start a food drive or work with a local charity to clean our beaches, bays, or waterways. You can volunteer at a local church. Don't belong to one? That's okay, but this year we are trying something new; go to church and tell them the truth, "I don't know where I stand with this whole God thing, but I am pretty sure it starts with service. Put me to work."

If you begin to live your life serving others, you will end up, by default, surrounding yourself with inspiring people.

For the month of May I would be remiss if I did not mention that the members of our armed services inspire me profoundly. These brave men and women selflessly put themselves in harm's way defending all of us. But service doesn't have to be that difficult. You know who else inspires me? The woman on the beach who, when walking her dog, picks up one piece of trash every day. *That* is inspiring!

You can be inspiring, too!

Reflections

WHO'S IN? LIST THE PEOPLE WHO INSPIRE YOU. LIST HERE WHAT *YOU* CAN DO TO BE MORE INSPIRING TO OTHERS.

NADIR

Nadir: *For the lowest possible level; lowest point.*

*H*ave you ever hit rock bottom? If not, have you come close? Or have you witnessed others hit it? I will tell you something about rock bottom that you may not believe. Rock bottom is completely individual and can be profoundly inspirational. Rock bottom can be the fifty-year-old woman who had a wonderful middle-class existence, part of the DINK (Dual Income No Kids) group of folks who get to spend money on vacations, jewelry, and cars that otherwise might have been spent on diapers, piano lessons, and college. She has lived her life exactly how she wanted and enjoys every minute with her spouse. But suddenly everything changes when her husband becomes ill and she loses her job.

Rock bottom can be the thirty-year-old mother who's just had her third beautiful child, but then four days after the birth of that child, she is informed that her baby is critically ill and will die before he leaves the hospital.

Rock bottom is that guy who was always the hit of every party. He was your drinking buddy in college, the best man at your wedding, and he was a huge success in life with a beautiful house and family and a great job on Wall Street. Then one day, a layoff leaves him daytime hours to do what he loves—drinking, just as he did in college. A year later he is still unemployed, his wife is filing for divorce, his kids won't speak to him, and he is in and out of rehab.

Rock bottom can be the woman who just spent a weekend in Puerto Rico and thought to herself, *Wow, the spicy food here is really bothering my stomach!* only to find out when she returns home that it wasn't the food, she has colon cancer. Did I mention this same person lost her husband just a year earlier and had thought *that* was her rock bottom?

Rock bottom SUCKS! I have been there, and I imagine you have, too. It is the bottom of a cave, where only the darkest and most nerve-wracking thoughts cloud your brain. It is the exact place where reality, fear, and pain collide, leaving you in a place of despondency. Often, when you think you've hit it, you are really just part of the way there; more than likely you still have a long way to go.

Don't hate me when I tell you that rock bottom can be the one place to truly find inspiration. *Rock bottom is defined as the lowest possible level.* I say *Rock bottom is a place from which you can only go up!*

Author J. K. Rowling was a single mother who had just lost her job when she began writing the award-winning *Harry Potter* series. Michael Jordan tried out for his varsity basketball team during his sophomore year and he didn't make it. Fergie, from the musical group The Black Eyed Peas (and now a solo artist), was addicted to meth and thought SWAT teams were following her prior to getting sober in 2001. I have to believe that these folks would not be where they are now if it weren't for rock bottom. Rock bottom is where you find a few very important things: you find out who your real friends are; you find what grit you are made of; and you find that when all is lost, you will *always* have hope. That is what you can find at rock bottom. If you search *really* hard, you can also find a bit of inspiration.

This might leave you scratching your head as you say, "Inspiration? At rock bottom? Are you one of those self-help nuts? Or are you just trying to fill pages?" Yes to both, ☺ but I also say I am not wrong. When you hit rock bottom that is the absolute *lowest* level. So your only choice is to search and find the inspiration you need to climb back up. What inspires you to move up from rock bottom? Sometimes, like in Rowling's case, it is your children. Other times, like in Fergie's case, it is a friend. Inspiration and hope, that is what can be found at rock bottom, when everything is cleared and stripped away. You must recognize that there is *always* hope, and then rock bottom can't trap you. Hope can make miracles happen and proliferate. Hope offers freedom, relief from pain, forgiveness—hope is everything. And when you combine hope and grit, those two things you have located at the bottom, they can make you soar to the top!

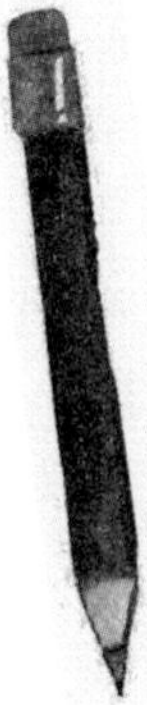

YOUR JUNE LETTER FROM THE PUBLISHER

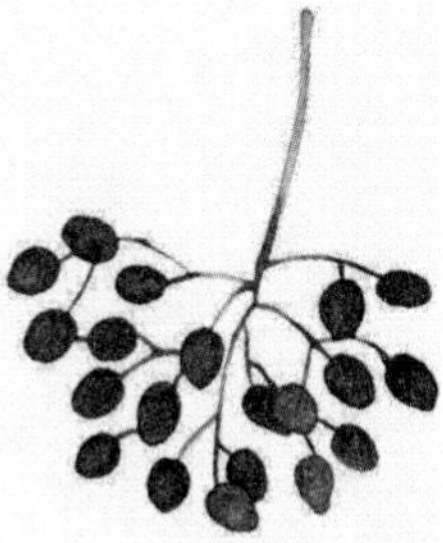

July

Jump for joy
Uplift others
Love yourself
You got this.

JUDGMENTAL

*Those who spend their time
looking for faults in others usually make
no time to correct their own.*

—Art Jonak

Judgmental: *a negative word to describe someone who often rushes to judgment without reason. The adjective "judgmental" describes someone who forms lots of opinions—usually harsh or critical ones—about lots of people. Judgmental types are not open-minded or easygoing.*

Mean People SUCK!

I received my first nasty reader phone message a few years back. It was quite a shock because the feedback I had been getting since becoming publisher of *Natural Awakenings Long Island* had always been wonderful. Readers had sent me emails, left voicemails, and posted Facebook messages saying how much they enjoyed the magazine. The message—which, honestly, is a cowardly way to confront someone—went something like this, "I don't believe in all this quackery (referring to advertisers in my magazine for yoga and meditation studios). He continued, "These centers are teaching communism." He went on (and on, and on) elaborating, and, in doing so, he eventually admitted he was "unsure what any of the advertisers actually do," thereby confessing that he was spewing opinions not based on any knowledge or fact.

He also complained that the advertisers "just want to make money," which I thought was funny because of course they do. Isn't that the reason we love America—or at least one of the reasons—because as a capitalist society we all have the ability to earn a fair living? Based on his tone, he should have been all for this concept. Isn't it actually a beautiful thing when our financial goals are tied into the betterment and health of our fellow man? Yet, this gentleman judged and spewed negativity on a subject he knew nothing about, and did it with an embarrassing amount of authority.

Humans judge—often harshly. It isn't enough that we judge, we then spew that judgmental negativity with absolute authority. I don't care how evolved you are, you know we *all* do it. Just one look at Facebook and you see strong opinions on subjects people know little or nothing about.

I am not innocent, I do it, too. It's . . . well, like I said, human. I am not sure how to stop judging people; I haven't figured that out yet. But it is very easy to stop *verbalizing* that judgment. Yup, it's simple. Just shut up! (LOL ☺) not really, but sort of yeah, really. Simply pause before you speak. Determine if what you are saying is positive or uplifting to someone or, heck, consider if it is even factual. Trust me, I don't always do this myself. If you are at my daughter's lacrosse game or my son's wrestling match, you may have heard me saying to a friend, "What is wrong with that referee?" (or that mom or that coach). Yes, I am judging. I want to stop judging, it's annoying, even to me (*ain't nobody got time for that!*). I am also positive our judging others verbally annoys the people around us. How about you? Do you want to stop the annoying back-and-forth arguments you have with folks on Facebook or at dinner parties that often starts with some form of judgment? If so, I may have a way to help.

I attended a seminar given by a contemporary thought leader, Panache Desai, and his response to anyone who makes a statement that he disagreed with was brilliant! He told us that if someone were to say something that you don't agree with, then you say out loud, "That is right!" while in your head you say . . . *for you*. So if someone says to me,

"You eat meat? I could never do that, it is murder!" I can say, "That's right!" and in my head I can say . . . *for you*. Someone says in that know-it-all-tone, "You know, kids have to be committed to just one sport at this age" (yes, people said this to me when my daughter was twelve and was—*gasp*—still playing three sports). In the past, I would defend her, myself, our decision, and the benefits of various sports. Now I realize that wastes too much energy. So instead, I whip out, "That's right!" out loud and then in my head . . . *for you*. What a great tool! This allows you to respect the journey of others without accepting that journey as your own. It also allows you to walk away from judgment and the act of being judged. It works in the reverse, too. Someone may tell me a decision they have made and I wholeheartedly disagree I don't have to say so. I can simply say, "That's right!" aloud, and in my head . . . *for you*.

The nasty caller was right in one respect because, at some point in that tirade, he said he was entitled to his opinion. The month of July we celebrate how wonderful and blessed our life is as Americans. We can add freedom of speech to the list of our blessings. Yet I challenge all of us to be even more conscious Americans, and to think before we speak. Pause and ask yourself, "Why am I saying this? What does it serve?"

Recognize daily, that what is good for you may not be good for others (and vice versa). Thus, the nasty gentleman who left that raging voicemail could have instead looked at the magazine and said, "That is right!" . . . *for those Commies*. ☺

Reflections

WHO DO YOU FIND YOU ARGUE WITH?
PERHAPS INCORPORATE A LITTLE
"THAT'S GREAT" INTO THOSE ENCOUNTERS.
TRY IT OUT AND JOURNAL THAT EXPERIENCE.

SELF-ABSORBED

You wouldn't worry so much about what others think of you if you realized how seldom they do.

—Eleanor Roosevelt

Self-absorbed: *Preoccupied with one's own feelings, interests, or situation.*

In most areas of the country, July is a month of vacations, holiday time, and exposing yourself to active pursuits. This could mean gardening, visiting beach towns, camping, and even more adventurous endeavors like trapeze, surfing, and CrossFit. Someone reading this might say, "Trapeze? Surfing? Just getting my half-naked body on a beach each summer is adventure enough!"

I wonder why we think that. When I was a kid, I would have been the *first* one on that trapeze or surfboard, and my bathing suit was simply a means to have summer fun. It was often a "hand-me-down," either too big or too small. I never cared because swimsuit was simply a conduit to all the adventure that was waiting for me, whether it was a beach, pool, sprinkler, or the Slip 'n Slide. (Which probably really should have been called Slip 'n Stitch because we all ended up with a laceration or two!)

What changed? What stops us now? Forget trapeze and bikinis; visually I can see what makes that a tough leap. But what keeps us chatting with other adults by a pool in the sweltering heat when all we really want to do is yell "CANNONBALL!" and jump in? What causes "inaction"?

Sometimes, the answer is honest enough at first glance—money, time, and lack of interest. Okay, that's fair, but is it the true reason you don't get involved in more activities?

I was asked to join a kickball league once by my friend Liz. I said, "No, sorry, too busy." Then I watched on Facebook as photos and statuses were posted, not about the scores or who failed to make a catch, but instead I clicked through images of women bonding, having fun, and laughing their asses off. When I was asked to join again this year, I explained that nothing had changed for me, I still didn't have time and I might miss a few games, but if that was okay, then I was in. I would play with the team BWB—short for Babes with Balls. It was only when I heard the name that I put two and two together and realized that what I didn't have last year, and what kept me from playing wasn't time—it was balls. Literally! I didn't have balls.

This year, though, I had identified and overcome what had really stopped me in the past: Fear of what I would look like on that field! Fear that others may think I wasn't good at the sport, or that I would cause a game-losing error. Can you imagine? Truth was I hadn't kicked a kick-ball since 1979. Forget about kicking one, how about catching one of those huge balls thirty-five years later? My mind raced with more fears of "what if." What if I looked stupid? What if I caused all the outs? Here I was, an adult raising two children and running my own business and a household, yet I was scared of what my friends and strangers would think if I caused outs in *kickball?* Seriously, when I look at this in print I wonder if I need some professional help. ☺

The only thing that kept me from the shrink's couch was the fact I knew I was not alone! You don't have to look further than the changing rooms near the swimsuits at Athleta to know that. Hearing women ask, "Does this make my butt look too big or my boobs look too small?" It's evident most women care what other people think. Instead of saying, "I will be playing volleyball or swimming on the beach. Who's gonna be able to see my butt with all my activity?" Or saying something even better, like, "Who cares what people think?" Perhaps the freedom to do this comes with the ability to realize *no one is thinking about you!* While I agree this executive function of caring that one doesn't look like an ass in public can sometimes serve us well in our decision-making process, (drunken Christmas parties anyone?) but for the most part this thought process is keeping us from a truly aware and experience-filled and, yup, I will say it, an *inspired* adult life.

First Lady Eleanor Roosevelt was controversial for her time because of her outspokenness, particularly her stance on racial issues. She advocated for expanded roles for women in the workplace, and the civil rights of African Americans and Asian Americans. While politicians and their spouses are typically hyperaware of their public approval ratings, Roosevelt didn't care what people thought about her. She says that's because she was acutely aware that "people were seldom thinking about her." Can I get an *amen?* This is so hard to grasp, especially in the narcissistic age of Facebook and selfies, but the truth is people are rarely thinking of us!

I will take it even one step further: if you are playing kickball, paddle boarding or, like me, are wearing a bathing suit that exposes more dimples than a Shirley Temple movie, then what people see is confidence—and that is hotter, more alluring, and attention-getting than tight abs and kickball skills. Besides, trust me (and Eleanor) when I say this: you would not care what people thought about you if you realized how seldom they are thinking about you.

This month, ask yourself, *What's holding me back from experiencing new athletic and healthy adventures?* If you feel the honest answer is, *I will look like a jerk, too fat, too silly, too* _____, then ask yourself this question: "To whom?" You will "*Look too* _____ _____ to whom?" Then remind yourself (firmly if you have to) that no one is thinking about you (or your Shirley Temple dimply ass! ☺). Rather than standing around the pool at a party in the oppressive summer heat gabbing, this summer take a running start, leap into that glorious water, and yell at the top of your lungs, "CANNONBALL!"

Reflections

LIST THE NAMES OF PEOPLE
WHO YOU THINK MAY BE JUDGING YOU,
STARTING WITH YOUR OWN NAME.*

*Cross the names below yours off the list and you are left with only you. Those other folks, they are busy living their own life, they aren't thinking about you.

_____

_____

_____

_____

_____

_____

_____

_____

_____

_____

_____

_____

_____

_____

_____

_____

_____

_____

_____

PRISON

As I walked out the door toward the gate that would lead to my freedom, I knew that if I didn't leave my bitterness and hatred behind, I'd still be in prison.

—Nelson Mandela

Prison: *A state of confinement or captivity.*

I was in prison for four days. Before you go thinking I am some sort of ex-convict, let me explain. One day, my niece and I went out surfing on my beach, which is located at the end of my block. I was excited to take her on a regular surfboard, and I could use my new eight-foot, stand-up paddle surfboard. I saw a small wave, not even a foot high, and we began paddling out to where the wave would break. There was only one other guy in the water, a man roughly ten years older than me. I smiled at him and said, "Good morning!"

He said, "Really? You are not going to surf right here, are you? Can't you go somewhere else? I mean it's kinda my wave." I was so shocked by this attitude I almost fell off my board. I looked around for cameras. Was I being Punked or was a Candid Camera crew hiding in the ocean? This guy wasn't *really* telling a woman and a sixteen-year-old beginner surfer not to surf "his wave" was he? And *What wave?* I thought. *It's barely a foot high!* He continued to complain that my teaching her could interfere with his surfing or that my paddle board—which was smaller than his surfboard—might "hold an advantage in catching a wave." There we were, in this *huge* ocean, just the three of us, and before the first wave rolled through he wanted us to leave. Not only did he want us to leave, he demanded it! I have seen thirty surfers in that same surf break in peeling, five-foot high waves figure out ways to share the wave. Yet he wanted the water all to himself.

Calmly, I reminded him, "This is God's ocean," and then less calmly, I asked, "Really? You are going to argue with me over a one-foot wave?" There we were in this beautiful, serene ocean about to throw down. I went at him. I wish I could say I practiced what I preached—illustrated some patience, tried to avoid judging, or turned the other cheek—but I didn't. I told him: 1) He didn't live in Long Beach (we all know each other here) so he could go surf another break if he had a problem with my niece; and 2) He was an awful person ruining what should have been a beautiful day shared by two people who were using surfing to bridge the age gap; and 3) He was an ASSHOLE! This last point seemed most rewarding.

But then, feeling uncomfortable by the vibe he was throwing out, I eventually paddled to a different break. To do so, I had to pull my niece out of the water and walk her somewhere else; it was silly and I was *pissed!* Super, super, shaking pissed! Not just for one day. The anger I felt imprisoned me for *many* days. I was held captive by it. My fury would not leave, and it consumed me so much that I even stopped paddle surfing for a few days. I would go up to my boardwalk and see a little wave and think, *Ah not in the mood.* It's probably pretty apparent to you by now that I was in a self-induced prison. All of my evolved pontificating flew out the window . . . I was seething.

I had to consciously free myself. If I didn't, I would stay in prison for who knows how long and—get this—that jerk would be my warden!

Are you in prison? If so, who or what is your "warden"? Is there a person in your life that you simply "can't forgive"?

Perhaps your prison is not ruled by a person that you are angry with but your own body. You have a disease that you face every day, and feeling ill makes you angry. Or maybe you have a disease that you faced and beat. Yet, even knowing that you have been victorious in your battle, you still hold anger against your body—your own cells—for failing you, for not protecting you. You are angry that you had to experience the surgeries or the medical procedures. That anger is your prison. The warden is your disease, your body, your memories, and sometimes your warden is just some strange guy surfing next to you. Cell or stranger, we must consciously free ourselves from the grip that they may hold on us.

Quite often, you don't even realize you are in prison. It is as if invisible bars surround you and stop you from conscious living. At times our anger is used to self-sabotage with angry self-talk that preaches against any form of self-improvement like, "Well, I am already so heavy, why eat healthfully now?" or "Food labeling is so confusing, I can't even begin to understand what's good for me—so pass the Doritos."

Author and blogger Pam Grout says that she "learned that consciousness creates the material world." A-MEN! If we want a world without anger, then we must consciously create one. It starts with us. I am not saying don't feel anger—that's ridiculous, and makes me angry just reading it. Anger is a necessary emotion, and letting go of anger is even more necessary. Together we must take baby steps each day to rid our lives of lingering anger. We must not let anger own us or, worse, dictate our behavior. Ridding ourselves of anger we hold inside can open us up to endless possibilities.

If Nelson Mandela can forgive his imprisoners so that he was able to live free, maybe it's time for us to start forgiving.

I hope I see that old surfer again, not so I can tell him off, but so I can tell him, "I am not angry with you." By doing this, I reinforce my own freedom.

And the truth is I am well aware that my own personal freedom, and the forgiveness I offer him, may also serve another purpose: to illustrate how un-evolved he is. And that may also get on his nerves just a little bit and maybe even imprison him! Win, win! ☺ (What can I say, baby steps, right?)

Reflections

WHO OR WHAT IS HOLDING YOU PRISONER?
WHO IS THE WARDEN OF YOUR ANGER?
WRITE THEM DOWN*:

*Now consciously release them.

_____
_____
_____
_____
_____
_____
_____
_____
_____
_____
_____
_____
_____
_____
_____
_____
_____
_____
_____
_____
_____

YOUR JULY LETTER
FROM THE PUBLISHER

August

*August is like
the Sunday of summer.*

CHOICE

*Never blame another person
for your personal choices—you are still
the one who has to live out the
consequences of your choices.*

—Caroline Myss

Choice: *An act of selecting or making a decision when faced with two or more possibilities.*

Disease is an individual journey and the treatment options are a personal choice. Take cancer, for example. There are a myriad of cancer treatments available using both Eastern and Western modalities. Cancer is alarmingly prevalent in the United States and is an equal opportunity destroyer of lives. We all know people struggling with it, many who have beaten it, and still more who lost their lives to it. My sister, Diana, died from head and neck cancer after years of treatment that combined chemotherapy, radiation, and surgery. Four months after her death, my husband, Kevin, was diagnosed with cholangiocarcinoma, a form of bile duct cancer. He was treated with a similar approach as Diana and also had a liver transplant. Ten years later, he is in complete remission.

When my husband was first diagnosed, we looked for something or someone to blame. People we came in contact with gave us plenty of choices: the government, big pharmaceutical companies, major corporations, his ancestors. But can it be that simple? Can all the bad things in our life, including cancer, really be someone else's fault?

As Americans, I believe perhaps we have some culpability. We live extremely stress-burdened lives as we chase the American Dream to an unattainable level. We work ourselves to the bone, which allows us to afford items such as fancy cars, big houses, boats, and often other extravagant things that we really don't *need*. We work so hard and so much. How about our diet? Our stressful lives have us running at such a frantic pace that we say there is no time to cook a healthy meal, yet, in the end we will blame McDonald's Corporation for the rise of diabetes? Nobody is forcing us into the drive-through on a regular basis to get the Big Mac combo meal. We are rushed, overworked, overscheduled humans and the majority of us eat crappy fast food, we don't make time for exercise, and we are so busy chasing the almighty dollar that even our personal relationships suffer.

This brings me to another toxic habit we have as a society. We place blame everywhere but on ourselves. We blame fast food restaurants (or our thyroid) if we are fat; the government or our parents if we are poor; our husbands and kids if we are unsatisfied; the school and the teachers if our kids get bad grades. We blame and guess what? That may be our biggest downfall because, when we blame others, we actually minimize our own personal responsibility for the situation. I am certainly not suggesting that Kevin, my sister, or anyone who is ill currently is to blame for their disease. What I am saying is that blame, as an emotion or as an action, is worthless. I will go one step further and say the simple act of blaming is dangerous. Instead of focusing on who is to blame for any tragedy you face, it may be wiser to focus on choice.

In his book *I'm No Hero: A POW Story*, Vietnam Veteran Charlie Plumb said that what helped him get through six horrendous years in a POW camp in Hanoi, Vietnam (known to those held captive as "The Hanoi Hilton"), was the knowledge that, ultimately, he had available to him *the power of choice*. "In a daily routine, or in a communist prison camp, each of us has the choice to succeed, to fail . . . or to become the

victim of circumstances." That quote, which I had heard more than fifteen years ago at a motivational speaking event, is what I recalled and
what anchored me when I faced both my sister's and my husband's diagnosis with cancer. Plumb was basically saying you will be faced with
circumstances and some will be absolutely horrendous, but the second
you blame others for the situation, you remove your own power to fix it.
If I wasted energy blaming doctors, corporate America, and our genetics,
then I was using the limited time available to me that I needed to actually
focus on the fight. And cancer, as you know, is one hell of a fight. When
Plumb was faced with his horrible ordeal he knew that he had choices.
Either he could succeed as a POW by surviving or he could become a
victim. The choice was his; he chose survival. What did surviving in a
POW camp look like? It was a bunch of small victories, like making a
deck of cards from slips of toilet paper (he said with authority, "It was
hard to shuffle."). Stuck living in an 8-foot by 8-foot cell, Plumb said they
had two choices: they could walk three steps, hit a wall, turn around,
and do it again; getting in a six-mile "walk" every day, or they could lie
in the corner, blame the government, the enemy, and eventually simply
die. "Victim or victor, that is *your* choice."

When my family members were ill, people said to me, "You are so
strong." Was I really? What choice did I have? Strong is choosing to turn
around and run into a burning building to save someone—to me that is
strength. My "building" was already burning; I just needed to choose to
pour water when and where I could and not burn myself in the process.
To not become a "victim of my circumstances." I promise neither my
husband nor I would have *chosen* to run into that "building." Yet we knew
we had a choice, victim or victor, controlled by fear or take control. We
allowed ourselves to cry, to grieve, and to feel self-pity—but only for a
brief time. Then we stopped blaming the world, the environment, and
God, and we got our buckets and began to pour water.

Illness for us became a fire-burning dance. There were multiple treatments, medications, and too many surgeries to count, all with their own
horrific side effects. It often seemed once one fire was out another reared

its ugly head. One "fix" often caused another problem, and at one point, we were in the hospital faced with the prospect of having him undergo a second liver transplant just one year after the first. We had no power over the flames. Yet we had power over our response to those flames.

If we get sick—and it's likely we *will* get sick—then we need to eliminate blame from our thought process. It serves no good purpose. "Adversity," says Plumb, "is a horrible thing to waste. If we waste the adversity by blaming other people for our problems, feeling sorry for ourselves, and denying that we have any control over our destiny, then we waste that opportunity that adversity gives to us."

Choice is what dictates our response; blame removes us from the responsibility of our response. Which of the two do you think is better for you?

This idea of blame and choice, I believe, is paramount to the success we will have in *both* good times and bad. I agree with Plumb when he says, "At the end of life, I imagine it would be just as meaningful to look back and say 'I tried' as it would be to say 'I succeeded.'"

Reflections

WHAT AND WHO DO YOU CURRENTLY BLAME FOR YOUR MISFORTUNE? PLACE IT HERE.

_____
_____
_____
_____
_____
_____
_____
_____
_____
_____
_____
_____
_____
_____
_____
_____
_____
_____
_____
_____

Release this and make a choice to take full control of your outcomes.

YOGA

None of my yoga pants have ever been to yoga.

Yoga: *A Hindu spiritual and ascetic discipline, a part of which, including breath control, simple meditation, and the adoption of specific bodily postures, is widely practiced for health and relaxation.*

Since menopause (yes, menopause, I was all done at around forty-four years of age), I have found that my fight-or-flight response is somewhat jacked up. I am a more extreme personality. If I am mad, I am furious; sad, I can cry a river; and happy . . . well at times I can feel almost a bit manic. I don't know if it is hormones or the lack of them, but I know that I am less than halfway through my life and my emotions are not something I want to lose control of.

You, too? Do you feel so overwhelmed at times that you are crying because of a television show? If it is *This Is Us*, that doesn't count! ☺ Do you find you are running so fast and so hard at work or throughout your day that you are on a perpetual hamster wheel? When you arrive home to your family is it becoming impossible to just hop off that wheel and be the mother, wife, or even roommate that you want to be. Do you find yourself reacting because there is no more milk in the house *(AHHHHH!)* or worse, no more milk in the house but there sure is an empty milk container in the refrigerator (please tell me it is not just my family)? In the end, the final straw that really makes me lose it will be the toilet paper. Yup, the toilet paper that mocks me as it sits smugly on our bathroom sink and not in the toilet paper dispenser, which is located roughly six inches from the sink!

You face big and little catastrophes every day. You might be firing on all cylinders when you come home to your six-year-old saying, "Mary said I am ugly," so it is only natural that you think to yourself, *Oh hell no! That kid better run when she sees me at the next class party!* Okay, that might not be natural, but I think you know where I am headed. In the twenty-first century we are going, going . . . GONE. We need to figure out how to come back. It used to be running for me, but with age came some aches and pains, and I find I can't run six days a week.

So how can we bring it back down? How can we breathe? How can we bring a sort of peace into our lives? A few years ago, I started practicing yoga. This was not because I was searching for peace; no I took up yoga because I was searching for awesome looking arms. (Come on don't judge! We talked about that!) A friend of mine who is in terrific shape said, "I do hot Vinyasa," when I asked her how she has such toned arms, and a day later so did I.

I became infatuated with it after taking a class with local yogi Kat Fowler who is beautiful in mind, body, and spirit. That first class showed me this: Yoga is a workout for the mind and body, and it is entirely about accepting and forgiving. Accepting and forgiving both our own limitations and those that we see in others. It is also about breathing through resistance.

The practice of yoga requires you to get into a pose and hold it for a period of time. The truth is you can go only so deep into a pose until you feel resistance. I am a type-A personality, and when I first started taking class, I would push—and push and push—when I felt resistance. Ego wanted me in that pose deep! It took a few years for me to learn that this wasn't yoga, and it was probably the opposite of it. The basis of yoga states that when you feel that resistance, the *only* thing you can—and should—do is breathe, not push.

When I first started to attend classes, they were typically a very athletic form of yoga, providing me with a strength-training and even cardio that I craved. I loved it; I loved sweating out toxins, and holding difficult poses. It helped. It calmed me. Up until the time my yoga studio changed disciplines. They moved away from "hot" and they started offering "warm" Vinyasa (That term is subjective; I mean I am freezing if it's 75 degrees!), and then they began to offer Gentle Flow. I have to be honest and tell you that last one brought me more anger then peace. Seriously, I would look at the schedule and *fume!* As a type-A personality, the yoga I was looking for was very athletic yoga. I mean, hello, I was attending these classes with the goal of hot-looking arms, not for a good nap! But I had no choice; I needed to do something, so I began to explore these classes. I went with resistance.

As a self-proclaimed uncoordinated fitness enthusiast (who knew there was such a thing?), that first class with Kat had opened me up to accepting both fitness and life challenges. Yet I began to realize it didn't make me less resistant. One day, I was in a warm, gentle Vinyasa (their words not mine) class and I was in a seated twist. I was jamming myself into the best twist possible, imagining my spine growing long, my organs being compressed, trying to force a sweat response that I felt I needed. The yogi leading the class came to me and said, "Do you feel that resistance?" *Ha ha! Do I feel that resistance? Of course I do! I am pushing through it like a champ!* I thought to myself. Then he said, "Yes, you do right? Okay now . . . breathe." I didn't realize I wasn't. Breathing that is. Not in this class, not ever.

I wasn't pausing to breathe at all, not when I was at work, not when I was with a friend, not even when I was being a parent. I didn't stop to breathe when I met resistance. Instead, I pushed back.

What resistance do you have in your life? Perhaps you are facing struggles with a teacher, or new manager, or coach. You go to work every day and you outperform others and that new monster, I mean manager, keeps pointing out things you don't do correctly. You don't stop to breathe, and you go back at her angrily. Or you're back at school as an adult and the teacher gives your paper an 80 when you believe it should be a 90. Breathe. Someone cuts you off on the road. Breathe. Your kids' school calls and "Mary" has pulled your daughter's hair or ripped her paper up. Breathe. Your yoga studio has changed its format and you fear you won't get from the new classes what you think you need. Breathe. Because if you take the time to breathe, you may find instead of getting what you want, "you get what you need." (So glad I didn't close out this book without getting at least one Mick Jagger reference). ☺

Yoga is individual; there are so many choices you are bound to find one that suits you. You make the decision what type of yoga practice you will participate in: Hatha, Bikram, Iyengar, and Vinyasa . . . the list goes on. There is a yoga practice out there for every one of us, from 2 years of age to 100. Try it! While yoga gives me a certain amount of both strength and flexibility, it has taught me something even more important, which is how to breathe in the face of resistance.

Yoga can be a metaphor for the life you lead. When you meet resistance in life—and you will, I promise—stop the struggle and breathe. After each yoga class I take, I find myself more willing to attempt other challenges in life that require forgiveness, acceptance, and letting go of resistance. Kickball league this fall anyone? ☺

Reflections

DO TEN MINUTES OF YOGA. HOW DO YOU FEEL? GOOD, NOW GIVE IT AN HOUR!

_____

_____

_____

_____

_____

_____

_____

_____

_____

_____

_____

_____

_____

_____

_____

_____

_____

_____

_____

_____

_____

_____

BALANCE

Some days you eat salads and go to the gym; some days you eat cupcakes and refuse to put on pants. It's called balance.

Balance: *A condition in which different elements are equal or in the correct proportions.*

"Isn't that bad for you?" my thirteen-year-old daughter asked me. She was sick, with what we'd find out was strep throat coupled with the flu, and we were on our way to the doctor. We were talking about gel nail polish, of all things.

"Probably," I replied. "Maybe," I corrected. "For some people," I stammered. "Jeez, I don't know anymore!" I laughed. The thing is, I don't. Do you?

We are a much more informed society today than we were in decades past when moms thought nothing of drinking cocktails while pregnant and smoking cigarettes in the car while their children sat seat belt-less in the back. Knowledge—that's good, and this information has protected us and has decreased the number of deaths and illnesses attributed to all of those things! Yay us! But it is getting to be a slippery slope.

Nowhere is that more evident than in the world of health and wellness. For example, there was a time when we all stopped drinking cows' milk and switched to soy. Ah, soymilk, poor misguided soymilk. Have you heard it is no longer the paragon of health? I've read it may actually be *bad* for you. So now if I go for the soymilk, after being bombarded by Internet/Google science, I might first pause and think *Is this bad for me?* The same might apply to gel nail polish, even regular nail polish, genetically engineered or non-organic fruit, sea water, tap water . . . and on and on and on. Isn't it *all* bad for us?

Breathe (not you, me . . . okay maybe you, too). Breathe, because science is ever-changing and the places we obtain our information are often not *truly* scientific. Times have changed. I will let you in on a publishing secret: paper is expensive, and as a magazine publisher and owner, it is my largest cost center. In the past, people would get their information from published journals. Those journals would not publish a scientific-based article without first making sure it was a good, large, randomized, double-blinded, placebo-controlled clinical trial whose results could be relied on to indicate truth for a larger population. Enter the Internet. Worse, the twenty-first century Internet where, with a few dollars'-worth of investment and some key words, "fact" becomes indiscernible from fiction.

It is overwhelming for the majority of us who are trying to live healthy lives and, more important, help our children lead healthy lives. I have a confession to make, I pack such a healthy school lunch for my son that he comes home starving every day, and I've found him in our "just for company" food cabinet so often that I am starting to believe I am doing more harm than good. Cucumbers, snap peas, a salad, some fruit, a half a sandwich (not too much bread, mind you). It isn't enough. I survived—maybe even thrived—on the steady stream of peanut butter and fluff sandwiches and Oreos dipped in Cool Whip. That was definitely not "good" for me but there has to be a balance.

It's not just my kids' diets; I have stomach issues, an irritable bowel is what they call it. I went to a nutritionist and she asked about my diet. I bragged. "A great day is eggs over asparagus, salad with almonds and shrimp for lunch, dinner is a broccoli and cauliflower casserole, and summer fruit!" I exclaimed with a bit of a smug smile on my face. Her answer had me dumbfounded, "No wonder you are in the bathroom all the time; too much roughage." Wait, what? I am afraid of bread (I mean what self-respecting, self-prescribing Google doctor like myself isn't?). Yet bread is exactly what she said I needed more of. Not a lot, but some. Balance.

I guess that's the answer I was looking for. When my daughter asked about gel nails, my answer was correct. All three of my answers were. The truth is, my mom had acrylic chemicals on her fingernails for a good portion of her life. She is eighty-five years old, plays golf three days a week and bridge the other days. That chemical crap she put on her nails didn't hurt her. In fact, I will go one step further and say, it made her feel good. She would get these nails done (seriously, living on Long Island in the 1980s, nails were important) and then she would go out to dinner every Friday. She loved those long nails, and when the diets she went on and off didn't get her where she wanted to be weight-wise and the hair color (yes that was a chemical dye, too) didn't come out the way she wanted, she always had her nails. They weren't bad *for her.*

Things are "bad for us." Everything seems "bad for us." It can be overwhelming. I believe this is where balance comes in. Living in a state where "everything is bad for you" can drive you crazy because it essentially means "nothing is good for you." That is NUTS! (Just heard the other day nuts are bad, too ☺.)

I think we all need to realize moderation is the key. If you deprive yourself of everything, I can guarantee you will be like me, ending your day with EVERYTHING (wine, Oreos, whipped cream combo is my favorite end-of-a-successful-day treat). So balance it out. Get your nails done if it will make you feel good; take the prescription antibiotics that were prescribed by a doctor for you (he is a doctor for goodness sake). And stop living in fear of life being bad for you and simply enjoy it. I think the only thing in this world that is truly bad for you is a life that is fear-based.

Reflections

ARE YOU LIVING A BALANCED LIFE?
ARE YOU DENYING YOURSELF SOMETHING
THAT YOU SHOULD, INSTEAD, SIMPLY LIMIT?
WRITE DOWN YOUR WORK HOURS AND
"PLAY" HOURS, UNDERSTANDING THAT SLEEP
IS ALSO A NECESSARY FORM OF PLAY.
DETERMINE IF THERE IS A HUGE
IMBALANCE IN YOUR LIFE.

YOUR AUGUST LETTER
FROM THE PUBLISHER

September

Hello, September.
Surprise me.

FORGIVENESS

*If you don't make peace with your past,
it will keep showing up in your present.*

—Wayne Dyer

Forgive: *To stop feeling angry or resentful toward
(someone) for an offense, flaw, or mistake.*

*Sometimes the first step to forgiveness is
understanding the other person is a complete idiot.*

—Bill Murray

You are headed into the homestretch. It is September already, you have been sticking with the ideas and challenges within this book, and we are headed toward the conclusion. Now it's about to get real. Forgiveness is easy to talk about but one of the most difficult things to offer.

Where I live, September signals the end of summer but also new beginnings. This month is also a somber one for New Yorkers, as well as for the rest of the United States, as it is the anniversary month of the most horrific terrorist act against our country.

Healing old wounds and embarking on new beginnings is an idea that probably goes more hand-in-hand than we realize. Honestly, how can you have a new beginning as a country, or as an individual, if you don't first heal your old wounds? You have room for only so much "stuff" in this life you lead. I truly believe that for every ounce of anger you release from your heart, you leave that space open for something better—love.

Let's be honest, though, there are people who have hurt you. BAD. There are things that happened that this author knows nothing about. *Who is she to suggest that I should simply forgive?* you may be thinking. I will tell you who I am. I am someone who also has had to forgive some pretty horrendous crimes. I'll go one step further and tell you truthfully that I am someone who has not been an angel her whole life and who, in her younger days, was at times downright mean. I am someone who needs to forgive and someone who needs forgiveness; we all do. My personal first step toward forgiveness was realizing that, in most instances, the offender was an idiot. (Yup, even when I was the offender.)

Let me break this down for you based on my own life. I had an experience in childhood where another child took advantage of my naivety and hurt me. For a very long time, I was *angry*—although not outwardly—deep, deep down in my soul, and I held on to that anger. As an adult I didn't think about it, but the anger toward my perpetrator and others who I felt let it happen persisted. As a child and well into my adult life I suffered from stomach issues. I had every test known to man every five years; I was sure that we would find some structural abnormality that could be causing the distress. I never thought to tie the ailment to the incident because consciously I believed the event was barely a "blip on my radar," or so I thought. I finally told myself, *Maybe you need to address this and forgive it. He was a kid and while it doesn't make it right you need to offer forgiveness.* So I did. It wasn't until I offered forgiveness in my heart to that person that my stomach symptoms and my life changed. Dramatically. (For a lot more on the topic of trauma and physical manifestations of pain later in life read Dr. John Sarno's book *The Mind Body Prescription: Healing the Body, Healing the Pain.*)

That forgiveness took work!

What about a time when I was an idiot? When I needed forgiveness? We are lying to ourselves if we live a life believing we have never done something wrong. I mentioned earlier that I went to camp in Massachusetts. I went for years and loved it. One year, when I was twelve, a new girl came to the camp named Sally. She was the "It Girl"! Sally was from "NYC" (so she said, later I realized it was Queens and not Manhattan, big difference), her skin was a golden brown color, and her hair was black with soft, long ringlets cascading down her back. She was also really funny—pee your pants funny! When I was with her I felt such giddy happiness. There was also another girl in my cabin named Marissa. She was not pretty, was overweight, and wore polyester clothing. She was also Sally's cousin. You might assume that Sally would be protective of her relative, but instead she teased Marissa relentlessly, and Marissa would laugh. It seemed like fun, so I joined in. I believed it was harmless, I mean Marissa was laughing right? I was young and stupid, and in retrospect I realize I was mean.

There was another girl that Sally perceived as "uncool." Her name was Alice and Sally couldn't stand her. I know now that this hate was purely based on jealousy, though I didn't have the experience or maturity to understand that back then. Sally was jealous of Alice because she was pretty and kind, and because Sally had recognized that I sort of wanted to be Alice's friend. Still, at Sally's urging, we played camp tricks on Alice, like hiding her clothes or telling a boy that she liked them. I had thought these were harmless pranks, that is until a counselor came to the cabin and told us Alice left camp early. Thirty-five years later my behavior still haunts me. I was young, I was unsupervised, and I was simply an idiot. A big, twelve-year-old idiot. Forgiveness thirty-five years later had to come from me. I needed to forgive the unsupervised twelve-year-old idiot. I have been angry—seriously disgusted—with that twelve-year-old idiot for years. Every time I thought about my behavior I would feel physically sick. I didn't think a public confession was necessary but perhaps it was.

I still haven't forgiven myself fully for that, which is interesting because I could certainly have forgiven someone else more easily than myself. What can I say? I am flawed, and one of my flaws is that I don't easily possess the ability to offer myself the forgiveness that I would easily offer another, but I am working on it.

What is forgiveness? It is the pure act of letting go of the anger. I am angry with myself for prior bad behavior. I need to get rid of that anger. We are angry with the terrorists for killing people we knew and people we didn't. We are angry about abuses perpetrated on us in childhood by adults or by other children.

We may be angry with our parents, siblings, abusers, bullies, even angry at the disease that stole someone from us. I challenge you (and apparently me) to forgive. Together, let's make the conscious decision today to let go of long held anger and replace it with forgiveness. Every ounce of forgiveness offered releases anger from our mind, heart, and soul and leaves room for so much more. This forgiveness thing can be hard for me. I am a grudge-carrying gal—always have been—and maybe you are, too. But recently I discovered a really important fact: forgiveness isn't the act of letting the other person off the hook; it is the act of letting *yourself* off the hook.

Reflections

WHO DO YOU NEED TO FORGIVE AND FOR WHAT?

_____

_____

_____

_____

_____

_____

_____

_____

_____

_____

_____

_____

_____

_____

_____

_____

_____

_____

_____

_____

NEGATIVITY

Your mind is the garden, your thoughts are the seeds.
The harvest can either be flowers or weeds.
—William Wordsworth

Negativity: *An attitude that is not hopeful or enthusiastic.*

often think people speak because they are afraid of silence. Sometimes (often) silence is much better than the spoken word.

Negativity is defined as an attitude that is not hopeful or enthusiastic. The definition alone should illustrate to you that you want no part of it. But often you can't escape.

I talk about yoga a lot; I guess it's because it is where I experience a good portion of my life. A few months back, on a snowy Tuesday, I took an amazing class that ended with a great meditation. The meditation grounded me, the yoga reminded me to breathe when feeling resistance, and I literally felt great. I rolled up my yoga mat with a peaceful ease, feeling ready to greet the day. That is until "Tank Top" (my nickname for a woman in the class who has all these cute tank tops) said, "Oh my God, this city SUCKS. I mean, seriously, I guarantee you won't even see a plow today."

Bam, there went my good feeling. I began thinking, *Will we not be plowed out? That has happened before. This city sucks? Does it? Will I be able to get to where I need to go? Will they plow?* There was only a half inch of snow on the ground, but Miss Tank Top's negativity had me preparing for the worst. My heart rate sped up and my palms got sweaty. Tank Top had stolen my Zen—bitch! ☺ The day ended with less than two inches of snow and everyone easily got to where they needed to go. But she had ruined my vibe with her negative, silence-filling chatter.

Fast-forward two weeks later to a different yoga class where Tank Top's nagging voice droned, "It's too hot in here!" Oh *hell* no! Do not mess with the temperature (which to me at 75 degrees was frigid). The studio used to hold 90-degree classes, yet now here she was complaining that the class listed on the schedule as "Hot Yoga" at 75 degrees was too hot? Again, I left feeling agitated.

You know these people; you may even be one of them. The people who fill silence with negativity just to be . . . interesting? Relevant? Engaging? I am not sure why people do it, but we are all guilty at one time or another. Someone tells us something and we put a negative spin on it. It becomes almost a habit. "Beautiful day out today" is met with, "Better enjoy it, gonna rain tomorrow."

The other thing that happens with negativity is it sucks you in. Like a vacuum picking up sand off your floors! (That's just a little reminder to myself that I need to vacuum; ☺) Truthfully, it is very easy to get sucked in. The woman at the yoga studio, Tank Top, wasn't alone in her bitching. People joined in on the bitchfest: "Yeah, this city never gets it right!" "Yup, we will all be stuck!" This is what I *don't* want to hear; not in the grocery store, not on the street, and *definitely* not after spending an hour and a half clearing my damn chakras!

Tank Top tried to engage me in her negative conversation as I was making my way out. I didn't take the bait—she annoyed me—and wouldn't even look up at her. That was my chosen response not necessarily because I was angry—okay, maybe I was angry—but because I believe that the less you respond to negative people, the more peaceful your life will become. Isn't that a main goal? To live a peaceful life? If it isn't . . . well, it should be. Still, I felt a bit mean not conversing with Tank Top, so before I left the studio I looked back and gave her a smile and said, "Enjoy your day!"

So what can we do when we are overwhelmed with exhaustive

whining, complaining, and negativity? When we are met with negativity, I think we need to do our best to ignore it. In fact, let's go a step further and rather than worrying about navigating someone else's negativity, let's put the focus on navigating our own. Sometimes, I find negativity slipping out of my mouth before I can stop it. I find myself filling the silence. Do you fill silence? To some extent we all do. This month, let's work on filling silence with something positive. Have nothing positive to share? Then fill that silence with something simple. A smile.

PLAY

And at the end of the day, your feet should be dirty, your hair messy, and your eyes sparkling.
—Shanti

Play: *To engage in activity for enjoyment and recreation rather than a serious or practical purpose.*

This guy I know, who I'll call "Kevin," is forty-eight years old and is a total "playa." I'm giving him a pseudonym because I'm not sure he wants the world to know this, even though it's obvious that he loves being one. The big, cocky grin on his face most days shows people that he truly digs his role. Oh, sure, it's a bit tough for me being friends with this player, but not for reasons you may think. Honestly, it's because I am jealous! I found myself many years back inspired by this Kevin's mentality! Thinking that maybe, just maybe, I should become a "playa," too.

Stay with me now. Kevin is a player. That is true. He plays volleyball, surfs, plays basketball with neighborhood kids, enters beach-wrestling contests—you name it. If there is some fun activity to join, some game to be played, Kevin is all in! I used to watch him with envy, angrily wondering: *Doesn't he have some sort of adult chore that needs to be done? A fence to be built or toilet to be fixed?* His friends often say, "Kevin knows how to enjoy every moment because he is a cancer survivor." That sounds plausible right? Except that I have known Kevin for more than twenty-five years—well before he ever faced illness, and he's always been a player.

I have another friend—let's call her "Jen." Jen used to play lacrosse in college, and she was good! She missed it in her adult life, and she wanted to play again but there was no league for her to join. With no team available to join, Jen created her own and then with no league to house the team, she created that as well. Jen can now be found playing lacrosse with other women at least once a week. Why don't more adults play like Kevin and Jen? Time is often a factor. We are parents, or we are caring for our own parents. We are business professionals or students. We are pet owners, homeowners, or home renters. We are the "uber busy" modern adult trying to do everything and be everywhere. So, yes, I would agree that finding time to play is an obstacle.

Another obstacle—maybe an even bigger one—is fear of embarrassment. Seriously, how would it look to see us chasing a kickball, playing in the waves, trying a new yoga pose, or shaking our booty in a Zumba class? But, come on, we are nine months in, we concurred that already didn't we? We are in a better place now, right? We are no longer giving a shit what people think about us because we have learned that most of the time no one is thinking of us. So then, what is stopping you from being a "playa"?

Inspired by Kevin, a few years ago I began to incorporate play into my life. First it was sporadically and with a bit of trepidation. Now it is much more a part of my life. I am not sure what people think when they see me trying to catch waves (with or without a board), kick (or miss kicking) a kickball, or trying to obtain side crow pose in yoga. But I don't care, because when I am playing, I am smiling—a great big smile—and when we smile, we are ageless.

George Bernard Shaw got it right some seventy years ago when he said, "We don't stop playing because we grow old; we grow old because we stop playing." If that is the case, then what are you waiting for? Fix the toilet tomorrow! Be a PLAYER! Play manhunt with your kids, kickball with your girlfriends, take a yoga class, play tag with your son, or Barbies with your daughter—or vice versa—just play! Get out there and join the other ageless adults who are playing. That's right, join the play revolution! And then, yes, you guessed it, come right here and tell yourself about your experience.

As for me? I have to make this letter short—I gotta go find a helmet because Kevin just asked me to go skateboarding!

Reflections

HOW WILL YOU INCORPORATE PLACE INTO YOUR LIFE?

HOW WILL YOU INCORPORATE
PLAY INTO YOUR LIFE?

YOUR SEPTEMBER LETTER
FROM THE PUBLISHER

October

Welcome, October.
Please be awesome.

CARPE DIEM

And in the end, it's not the years in your life that count. It's the life in your years.

—Edward J. Stieglitz, MD

Carpe Diem: *To seize the day.*

*Twenty years from now you will
be more disappointed by the things you
didn't do than by the ones you did do.
So throw off the bowlines.
Sail away from the safe harbor.
Catch the trade winds in your sails.
Explore. Dream. Discover.*

—Author Unknown

This advice, often attributed to Mark Twain, is responsible for launching my adventure, starting my own company and what ultimately pushed me to take the leap to become a publisher of a health magazine. No, I didn't read the quote one day and decide to dive headfirst into a new career. Rather, the sentiment has accompanied me through life to use when I was looking for a little courage to take on something new. You see, I am often ruled by fear. Reading this book you may not believe that. Remember, though, that this book was for me first. To move me from my comfort zone and into a more inspired way of living. Sometimes we all live life a bit fear-based. For example, I will see a class, let's say a hula-hoop class, that looks fun and maybe even hilarious! Why wouldn't I just sign right up? Vacations are the same; while I dream about a trip to Panama or Mexico, the naysayer inside says to me, "Nah, the water in those countries may make you sick, or worse, what if there are banditos?" (Obviously, I have the capacity to ratchet up my fear base to an entirely crazy level.)

The thought of taking a hot yoga class should be an easy decision for me, right? After all, yoga is a recurring theme in this book. Yet, way back for the first class, I needed Mark Twain's advice to do it. Yup, it's true, for my first Bikrahm yoga class, I needed inspiration to be locked in a 105-degree room with fifty sweaty, middle-aged men and woman in various states of undress for ninety minutes while we bend "back, way back, way, way back . . ." "OH MY BACK!" Why? Because, I am fear-based: a Nervous Nelly at times ☺. So the opening quote is my go-to words of wisdom to help move my decisions out of their natural fear-based response, which is usually "no." Oh, I am not that rude when asked to participate in a bubble soccer league (Yes, there is such a thing. No, I have not said yes to it yet.) or even an exotic surf trip, something I would desperately love the courage to say yes to. I simply find a reason to say "no" that doesn't look fear-based. "Sorry, we have kids' sports." That one is a good answer now that my children are in school and, yes, their sports commitment is larger than my commitment to my job at times. But I let my kids' sports become my way out. When the sports are over, I am sure I will have another excuse for not doing something: "no time," "no interest" (even when I am interested), etc.

Would you believe I suffer from a second serious condition along with my fear-based decision-making syndrome? I suffer from something I call FOMO: Fear of Missing Out, which can be a real motivator. The idea that you regret only "the things you didn't do" has always stuck with me and often provided me with a bit of courage.

We each play many roles throughout our lifetime. I am wife to Kevin; daughter to Marilyn and Ray; mother to Dylan and Reagan; sister to Diana, Lana, Caroline, and Laurajean; aunt, yogi, chocolate lover, gym rat, wine lover, couch potato, Zumba enthusiast, potato chip sneaker, PTA member, friend, Long Island local, paddle surfer, sugar craver, green drink maker, runner, and now *(gasp),* author.

Every one of those roles is a bit scary (honestly have you met my family?). It is scary to give of yourself and scary to try new things. *Life* is scary! Taking a leap is scary, but isn't missing out scarier? I believe if you asked Kevin, he would say "yes."

As a mother of two beautiful children, I've often relied on this inspirational quote, while encouraging my children to try something new, make a new friend, or when encouraging them to engage in a new sport or academic activity.

We want to regularly nurture our spirit, but often fall on the excuses, "Oh, I'm too busy to do *that* today." That is a fear-based excuse. You are only fooling yourself when you say this. We *have* time for what we *make* time for. It is true that you don't have time. Time is not endless, it is finite (don't look so shocked, remember I broke the news to you this February about your impending death). So spend what time you have wisely. You don't want to look back and see that you didn't use your time to its full potential. We have to use our time to love with abandon, to tackle fears, and launch into careers and hobbies not *without* fear but *in spite* of fear.

So let me ask you, what is being proposed to you right now? A new relationship? A new career or opportunity? A new adventure or hobby? What is fear keeping you from? Whatever it is, tell yourself, "It is time to sail away from the harbor."

Reflections

WHAT ADVENTURE AWAITS YOU? WHAT ARE THE STEPS YOU NEED TO TAKE TO "SET SAIL?"

_____

_____

_____

_____

_____

_____

_____

_____

_____

_____

_____

_____

_____

_____

_____

_____

_____

_____

_____

MEASURED

*The true measure of your worth includes
all the benefits others have gained
from your success.*
—Cullen Hightower

Measure: *To ascertain the size, amount, or degree of
(something) by using an instrument or device marked in
standard units or by comparing it with an object of known size.*

*I*n Jonathan Larson's Broadway play *Rent,* at the end of the show, is
a cacophony of amazing voices singing about, of all things, time in
the song "Seasons of Love." The actors explain in song that a year
can be defined as 525,600 minutes, but then they question how do you
measure it? How do you measure a year? Do you measure in daylights or
sunsets, midnights or cups of coffee? In inches or in miles or in laughter
or in strife? Then the answer comes from some angelic voice, when she
belts out, "How about love? Measure in love!"

Ha! Wouldn't that be rich? If only we were wise enough to measure
a year in love!

Humans are notorious for trying to find a magical tool to measure
success. Something that validates them, allowing them to say, "Yes, I am
successful at my new job." The career measuring stick most use? Money.
How about measuring your success as a parent? If our children eventually become doctors or lawyers, we'd likely feel that we were successful

as parents. Finance, status, bragging rights, these are all our measuring sticks. All too often, success is measured in the money we make, as exemplified by the things we buy to show that we've made a lot of money. That's probably why there are so many expensive cars on the road today. Status indicates success, success gives you status, and the two are measured by the almighty dollar.

Five years ago, in the month of October, I took some of my own great advice and "set sail." I purchased a magazine and formed a company. Three weeks later, Superstorm Sandy tore through Long Beach, leaving a trail of destruction in its wake. Sandy flooded my new office with sewage, destroying everything I had just purchased. It was all gone: the existing contracts, computers, software, and the first month's issue of the actual magazine. Did I mention this office of mine was in my house? Yes, and a third of my home was ruined and would need to be gutted to the studs. Worse than my home status was that of my neighbors' homes. I was lucky that only part of my house had been destroyed; others in my town were not so lucky, and many faced total loss. Rebuilding parts of my home and office was a long, mostly torturous process of insurance denials (they covered the house but not its contents) and apologies (for not covering the contents), in that order, and construction workers who showed up when they could.

The year after the storm, I had no choice but to continue with that leap of faith and launch my magazine, while in the midst of gutting my home, fighting with the insurance company, and calming my children's fears. Maybe it wasn't as great a launch as I had planned originally. Measured in financial terms it was not a success and, following similar logic, neither was I. Ugh! I am competitive and I want success! We all do. But what if I had been using the wrong ruler? Instead of looking at my company financials and the stacks of bills, what if I measured my success using love as the yardstick and not money? Everything is different from this perspective. When I look back at the aftermath experiences of that storm measured in love, then all I see is success! I see people bringing clothes, food, and Red Cross blankets; neighbors and strangers helping to tear down drywall from flooded homes, and sharing generators and gas. I can only seem to remember that I witnessed a beauty in humanity after the storm that I never would have experienced had the storm not occurred. I have a choice how I remember and measure that storm, how I measure that new business or my first year of marriage. Choose to measure in love.

Here is what happened when I looked back on 525,600 minutes of my new career as an author. I hated the pressure but love the book. Deadlines were tough, but I loved the process and working with the amazing Christine Belleris. I needed to skip out on a few things that I didn't want to miss while writing this book, but I love, love, *love* my husband for making breakfast and lunch for the kids, and I love my kids for encouraging me. I loved the experiences that I had as I ventured deeper into a more inspired lifestyle. And my magazine readers, and friends, who texted and emailed me with encouraging words and inquiries on when and where they could purchase the book? I love them. I have no idea how much money this book may—or may not—bring in. But am I measuring my success as a first-time author with a financial measuring stick? Oh, no, I am measuring it in love.

During these past 525,600 minutes, what else did I love? I loved sunsets, from Long Beach to Fire Island; I loved my kids' surf contests, wrestling matches, and lacrosse games. I loved surfing in my "backyard" where I would often encounter new friends (and even dolphins!). Oh, and I loved my wedding anniversary. Sure, there were things I hated. Things like the passing of someone dear to me, and the wakes that I had to attend. But I love that I was able to say at those wakes, "I had the opportunity to know and love that person and that my minutes with him or her were so amazing they were immeasurable."

Jonathan Larson died young and tragically. I bet, though, that were he to have the opportunity to measure that year prior to his death, working on a piece of art that filled his soul, he would say, his 525,600 minutes prior to his death were absolutely "a success!"

Reflections

WHAT IS YOUR MEASURING STICK?
WHAT ARE YOU MEASURING?
(LOOKING FOR A LITTLE INSPIRATION?
ASK YOUR ALEXA DOT OR SIRI TO PLAY THE SONG
"SEASONS OF LOVE" FROM *RENT*.)

REFRAME

*Attitude is the ability to reframe the experience
to empower you to future victories.*

—Orrin Woodward

Reframe: *To frame or express (words or a concept or plan) differently.*

*The voyage of discovery is not in seeking new
landscapes but in having new eyes.*

—Marcel Proust

"Y ou gotta reframe that!" said fellow publisher Joe Dunne one day when I was complaining about my feelings toward a business associate. The relationship had begun to feel one sided. "I can't stand it; there is nothing more I can give. I feel used!" I complained. My expectation was that Joe, a good friend, a man I admired for his spunk and his wisdom would sympathize with me and maybe give me a salty word or phrase to hurl at this person. Instead, he simply said with his raspy Rockaway Beach inflection, "Come on rock star, you gotta reframe that thought!" Joe made me think. He usually does.

When things occur in our lives, they don't have an impact *on us*. Rather, they elicit reactions *from us*. Unpleasant events happen in all of our lives, but it is the way we hang that event on the proverbial wall of our life—how we "frame" that event—that determines its impact on us.

Take, for example, the employee who gets a bad annual review, or the student who receives a bad report card, or the multitasking adult who is both a student and an employee who receives a bad review and at the same time a bad report card! (Poor sod.) They have the ability to frame it as an opportunity for growth and development, to implement changes to ensure that next year is even better. That type of frame is what I would refer to as a Frame of Empowerment. That frame gives you a source of positive energy that propels you toward a specific goal. These positive actions then fuel your very cells, your relationships, and your whole life. You can also choose to frame events in your life with what I like to call the "FU frame." That approach is used when you place the things that are happening to you in a F&*k You Frame. Yes, that is one angry frame. That was the frame I was using in the above scenario with my friend Joe. Using this frame for an event only spurs you to begin fighting. Fighting your bosses and the teachers, it initiates you into a gossiping frenzy about the review you got at work, telling your co-workers month after month that your manager is "fat and stupid." It stirs, if you will, a shit storm around an already unpleasant event. The truth is that the FU frame entertains others, but it leaves you with the life chaos. The only person that particular frame actually "F's" is YOU!

Everyone should have a friend like Joe: an older, wiser, full of pep "guru" who will set you straight when needed. He made it clear that it wasn't what was happening to me that caused my unrest, it was how I viewed or "framed" it.

This is true for physicalities as well. Too often, I have heard women my age speak with disgust, about "bat wings" on their arms, "love handles" draping their hips, and wrinkles on their faces. A much more loving approach is to simply eat healthfully and exercise, and when you believe you are the healthiest version of you, then reframe and see your body as the thing a child hugs at night when running from monsters under his or her bed. Your wrinkles? Reframe those beautiful suckers as etchings that are permanent reminders of all the times you have loved and laughed, smiled and winked.

I would *never* be writing this book if a company that I had dedicated my life to for over thirteen years hadn't laid me off. The day I was laid off, I was devastated and angry, and I did gossip with my friends. I called my friends and co-workers, crying, saying that the man that made the decision to let me go was "fat and stupid." And, at the time, I think I even called him "lonely"! (Don't judge, I was hurt. ☺) In the end, though, after I grieved for a day or two, I reframed my situation as an opportunity instead of a catastrophe (even though it kind of was at the time).

In 2012, Oprah said the following statement that literally helped me change the way I live my life (when I remember it). ☺ When she discussed the abundance in her life, she said, "I live in the space of thankfulness and I have been rewarded a million times over for it. I started out giving thanks for the small things and the more thankful I became the more my bounty increased. That's because what you focus on expands, and when you focus on the goodness in your life you create more of it."

So what if I "reframe" my initial thoughts (thank goodness for friends like Joe!) and live in a state of gratitude instead? Would my bounty increase? Could it possibly be that easy? By simply changing the way I view the world, reframing my thoughts with gratitude, would my life be different? I guess it can't hurt to try, and let's face it, I mean, *hello?* Oprah has accumulated a pretty impressive bounty!

Here it goes: I am grateful for wonderful parents whose love and support continues to yield infinite blessings, and for four amazing sisters—two that are my angels in heaven and two that are my best friends here on Earth. I am grateful for my friends who are my soul sisters and my children who make my heart sing every time they laugh. I am grateful for my cousins, and my in-laws (yup, I said it—my in-laws—they rock!). I am grateful for plank pose and headstand and family near and far. I am thankful for nieces and nephews who as they age become my friends, for my fabulous neighbors, my mentors old and new, and a husband whom I fall in love with again every time he smiles (in an effort to be transparent, when I am not falling in love with him, I am undoubtedly bitching at him about something). I am thankful for waves (and dolphins!). I am thankful for the ability to write. I feel blessed when my legs and arms run those races that my mind wants to quit. I'm grateful for my Catholic faith and the hard times it has seen me through. I am overwhelmingly grateful for the blessing of having known and expressed love and laughter with so many who have left this world entirely too soon. I am especially grateful when I glimpse a hummingbird in my garden.

Hmmmm! That felt good, really, *really* good. What if I did that every single day? What if, like Oprah, I simply focused on being grateful for what I have? What if I stopped focusing on an opportunity missed or an item lost and replaced those thoughts with gratitude? Already, I have experienced even more wonderful blessings come my way. I'll give you one more what if. What if we all did that? What if we all focused on gratitude? What would the collective universal bounty be then?

Reframing led me here, where I sit doing something I love and would never have had the opportunity to do had I not first been laid off. I can honestly say I am grateful to that stupid, fat, lonely man! ☺ (Again . . . baby steps!)

Reflections

**DESCRIBE A CURRENT SITUATION
THAT YOU SHOULD REFRAME.
CAN YOU REFRAME IT WITH GRATITUDE?**

YOUR OCTOBER LETTER
FROM THE PUBLISHER

November

It was November—the month of
crimson sunsets, parting birds, deep,
sad hymns of the sea, passionate
wind-songs in the pines.
Anne roamed through the pineland
alleys in the park and, as she said,
let that great sweeping wind blow
the fogs out of her soul.

–L. M. Montgomery

THANK YOU

Thank You: *A polite expression used when acknowledging a gift, service, or compliment, or accepting or refusing an offer.*

"Thank you" is powerful. It holds in it gratitude and creates a space for empathy. But I will tell a little secret about "thank you." It holds a certain freedom.

I have a bad habit. If I am mad, I am *mad!* I tend to take things perhaps too personally, and in the end, I react. STRONGLY! At times, perhaps I even overreact. It might be to things like my sister telling me she didn't like my haircut; a guy cutting me off on the road; a lady cutting in line at the grocery store. Trust me, I have a few choice words for those folks! "Oh no you *didn't!*" (Imagine a super head circle with those words and some real strong puckered lips.) Ah, come on, I know you are guilty of it, too. I have had enough middle fingers thrown at me in my lifetime to know that I am not alone in my anger-based responses to situations! I imagine many of you reading this may share a similar proclivity.

Two months ago, I decided to replace angry words with a simple "thank you." Yup, anyone who pisses me off this week is getting a thank you. That's what I told my husband, Kevin. "No way! You can't do it and it won't bring you satisfaction, it simply won't work," he said, to which

I replied with a smirk, "Thank you!" Ah, hell yeah, I love a challenge! And so it began. My Thank-You Experiment went something like this: if someone cut me off, I did *not* throw a middle finger; instead I waved and pleasantly said, "Thank you." A car beeped at me for sitting too long at a green light? "Thank you," mouthed in the rearview mirror with a smile. Thank you is a diffuser. It is not always easy, and I will not lie and say I am always successful remembering to bring it out in replace of my middle finger; however, when I do remember, it actually feels . . . AWESOME!

One particular day, Kevin was a firsthand witness to me employing the "thank-you magic" when we were riding our bikes with our kids on the boardwalk that extends out to Fire Island. A couple on the path yelled, "You know you aren't supposed to ride on this part of the boardwalk! Jeez, don't you know anything? My God, can't you read?"

What a great day we were having, sun shining, our kids laughing, only to be interrupted by these two a#@ holes yelling at us and, worse yet, questioning my ability to read! I wanted to scream, "Mind your own business, jerks!" Instead, I rang my bike bell—*ding, ding*—and said, you guessed it, "Thank you." The funniest part is that Kevin, who was riding behind me, saw their disappointed faces. He chuckled, telling me that when I thanked them nicely, they literally didn't know what to do. They were shocked and dumbfounded. They continued to walk on, but, according to Kevin, the dissatisfaction on their faces was priceless. He overheard their conversation, which he repeated to me: "Did she just say thank you?" and the other said, "Thank You? Idiot!" I peddled away with a smile. A BIG smile.

In this situation, it wasn't just about getting the last word or being "cheeky." The truth is, I set a good example for my kids to model. My daughter even asked, "Did you say *thank you* to them?"

"I sure did, honey, they told me information that they thought was necessary for me to have." This is so much better than explaining why mom was screaming at two strangers. If my kids weren't there it still would have left me smiling; no other word exchange could have done that. I peddled away with a tremendous smile on my face.

Thank you has all the wisdom, forgiveness, and inspiration you need. And thank you can absolutely contain a dash of f**k you! That's it: thank you can be the new f**k you!

This letter is a short one; there is a reason for that. I understand we are entering the holiday season and Lord knows you are busy. But another reason this letter is a bit short is because there isn't more I can say on the subject. I simply ask you to give it a try. "Thank you!" Actually, I *insist* you try it out. These two words can be loads of fun! You will literally change the way an exchange is about to go and end with a much more peaceful feeling. There's an added bonus for those of you who, like me, are not yet 100 percent "evolved." By employing the "thank-you project" we'll still get the last word in an argument! ☺ Thank you!

Reflections

TRY THE THANK-YOU PROJECT WHEN SOMEONE TRIGGERS YOUR ANGER. WHAT HAPPENED? HOW DID IT MAKE YOU FEEL? WHAT WAS THE REACTION OF YOUR RECIPIENT?

LUCK

Luck is believing you're lucky.
—Tennessee Williams

Luck: *Success or failure apparently brought by chance rather than through one's own actions.*

I attend Mass every Sunday. There were times when I would miss a few weeks at a time but recently, over the last seven years, we have had an insightful priest and I enjoy sitting for that hour and hearing him speak and reflecting in prayer on the thoughts expressed in his homily.

This letter is based on one of Father Brian Barr's homilies, and it inspired me and forced me this November to consider luck.

WHAT I LEARNED FROM A TAOIST TALE TOLD BY AN IRISH PRIEST

This farmer had only one horse, and one day the horse ran away. The neighbors came to console him over his terrible loss. "Oh, this is so terrible," they all cried. The farmer said, "What makes you think it is so terrible?"

A month later, the horse came home—this time bringing with her two beautiful wild horses. The neighbors became excited, stating how happy they were for the farmer's "good fortune." Such lovely, strong horses! The farmer said, "What makes you think this is good fortune?"

Many weeks later the farmer's son was thrown from one of the wild horses and broke his leg. In this state he could no longer work the farm for his father. All the neighbors were very distressed. "Such bad luck!" they all cried. The farmer asked, "What makes you think it is bad?"

A war came, and every able-bodied man was conscripted and sent into battle. Because he had a broken leg, only the farmer's son remained. The neighbors congratulated the farmer. "This is good luck you have had," they all said. "What makes you think this is good?" said the farmer.

You see the farmer knew something that most of us have a hard time conceptualizing. There is no luck, not good and not bad. Just randomness.

When experiencing a situation, it is hard to know on what side of luck you have landed. What situation is good and what situation is bad. Is it bad luck to find out you have cancer, or is it good luck because it has been found? Is it bad luck to have been laid off, or is it good luck because you needed a push to take a new path (and to get away from that horrible jerk of a boss)? Who's to say? Rather than guessing at what is good luck and what is bad luck and trying to discern what we should be grateful for and what we should be pissed off about, why not be grateful for all of it. I just chuckled a bit because I think I got on my own nerves with that statement ☺. But hold on and let me take you through what may seem like an annoyingly Pollyanna-ish statement. How do we know what is good and what is bad? There are countless people who, by facing some tremendous tragedy, have persevered and managed to change the trajectory of their lives for the better. I am certain, if you ask them, they will tell you they are thankful for their blessings and their adversity—both of which led them to the lives they lead today. A few months back we spoke about JK Rowling, Michael Jordan, and to a much lesser extent Kelly Martinsen (who would not be typing these words if it wasn't for "luck").

Let's try an experiment—oh, how I love experiments this month! This Thanksgiving, while we focus our energies on gratitude for the blessings in our lives, let's go one step further and find it in our hearts to give thanks for the seemingly "bad luck" in our lives. Find a small blessing that exists within the job loss, the divorce, even the disease. Recognize that perhaps, somewhere, somehow, this bad luck will lead to something beautiful, and then let it! Let that gratitude free you from the control this bad event may be holding over you, and let this freedom carry you onto the next stone on your path.

If you are facing something devastating right now, I can imagine that my words can draw an almost angry reaction at this advice. I cannot say it enough, "I get it!" (Kinda makes me angry just writing it.)

I need to share a bit more about myself, so that you don't get *really* mad at this letter, especially if you face life-threatening disease or worse. In 2007, my husband was diagnosed with cholangiocarcinoma, and even after chemo/radiation and a liver transplant, he faced the potential loss of that new liver, multiple times, over a period of roughly three years. The same year that my husband first learned he had an autoimmune disease that would later turn into cancer, my son was diagnosed with Landau Kleffner, a rare seizure disorder that robbed him of the comprehension to utilize speech to communicate. So, yes, I have seen my own share of shit! No, I was not always grateful, sometimes—most times—I was pissed off! But there were days, and moments, that I was. I was grateful for the one medical resident who saw Dylan have a seizure and chose to admit him to the hospital, which began the path of healing. Grateful for the time when, so saddened by my son's and my husband's diseases, that the four of us "hid" in our house in a dark room watching movies and eating pizza. I am grateful for the empathy that my daughter Reagan has because she lived through those experiences. I am grateful for some very small and some very big things that occurred during these years. And that brief feeling of gratitude may be just what I needed to keep going, to keep the stress of these problems from wreaking havoc on my own health.

There is randomness in our lives that we can't control, and like a wise priest once told me when he shared a Taoist Tale, we can't truly determine: "What is luck?"

So perhaps we need to accept a certain amount of randomness in our life, and, where possible, find a bit of the good in even the worst luck.

Reflection

DEFINE YOUR BAD LUCK. SEARCH FOR THE GOOD LUCK WITHIN IT.

_____
_____
_____
_____
_____
_____
_____
_____
_____
_____
_____
_____
_____
_____
_____
_____
_____
_____
_____
_____
_____

KINDNESS

In a world where you can be anything, be kind.

—Unknown

Kindness: *The quality of being friendly, generous, and considerate.*

re you kind? Be kind. Seems simple, right? You might be thinking, *Oh my God, did she say be kind? I mean* obviously *I am kind.* I get it; it seems cliché, annoying, and even obvious. But can you tell me you are always kind? I mean really and truly every single day in every single situation, are you kind?

Your child walks through the door with a bad grade, you watched him refuse to study, you want to ring his neck, how can you be kind? Your toddler walks in and tells you "Sally" just hit him in the head with a stick. Are you kind to Sally (or to her mother ☺)? The coach didn't play your daughter the entire game. The neighbor blocked your car and now you are stuck in your driveway. I could go on and on about the daily offenses that happen to us, and I have to ask you, are you kind then?

I am not. I wish I was, but no, I am not *always* kind. My kids, they hear a lecture that often starts something like, "How do you expect to get into college, with those grades?" Not kind. "Sally" is left unscathed (I mean I am not a barbarian), but her mother will get an earful, trust me, and that is not kind. The coach, oh the coach . . . (well, honestly, he is safe because if I open my mouth he will play my child even less if that is possible!). The neighbor will get a nasty note on his car! All of these situations require a certain amount of kindness that, to this date, I have not truly been offering. You can be mad or disappointed and still be kind. In fact, I will take it one step further and say you *absolutely* must be kind when you are mad.

I did an experiment. For twenty-one days, I randomly changed mad to kind. At first it was annoying. When I am pissed, I *want* to be pissed, I *need* to be pissed. But after the first few times, it was . . . interesting. The first person to experience this "kindness" was a friend. She is needy, often anxious over the same little things, and at times demanding. I sometimes get frustrated with her. She texted me with a crazy demand (yes, I said demand) and normally I need to set her straight, which backs her down and gives me a sense of peace. Instead, I looked at the demand and then I kindly repeated it to her, "Sorry, just to be sure you are angry and are demanding that I go to dinner with you despite the fact that I just explained I have my daughter's last lacrosse game to attend?"

I wanted to first clarify, in writing; is that truly an offense? Then I validated her feelings. I mean to me she is nuts in her manner and assumptions, but she doesn't have children of her own so perhaps me blowing her off for mine adds insult to injury, so I wrote back kindly, "Okay, that's okay, I hate that you feel that way." *Hmm,* silence on the other end of the phone as she normally gets a fight back from me. Eventually, she tried again. And again, I said, "I hate that you feel that way." The situation was dropped, we had dinner the next night and, what's more, we had fun!

My teenager, who came home with repeated bad grades (read F), well let me tell you that one was tough. You got a 55 on a test that I continually begged you to study for? *Kindness,* I thought to myself. Honestly what I really yelled in my head was, *SERENITY NOW!* (But not sure how many would get the *Seinfeld* reference.) I said, calmly, "That stinks, bud, I know you aren't happy with that. I know you have goals to go away to college, and it's important to you, so how can I help you to attain those goals?" Oh, I still took away his phone, but what I also took away was the high-pitched, bitch-fit that usually would occur in my house.

Service to others is an amazing way to be kind and to keep kindness at the forefront of your life.

I believe service is one of the hardest things to participate in but absolutely the most rewarding. I mentioned a few letters back about my friend the local wrestling coach. It is good to be friends with him because he has time for *everything*. If you need him, he is there, no questions asked. He is *busy*, working more than one job, planning a wedding (to a woman whose soul is as beautiful and giving as his), and managing more than one wrestling team, but if one of his boys needs him, he drops everything and will be there. It is absolutely humbling how kind he is and how available. When I catch myself saying, "I can't go to the fundraiser," or "sorry no time for coffee," I think of him . . . and I make the time.

So there is my friend Miguel, who absolutely and completely lives his life in service to the young men entrusted to his care. He is kind. He doesn't seem to know the words, "No I am too busy." He works multiple jobs, he is available whenever someone needs him, and he is never too busy to open his heart or his home. I swear his "kindness" and his service literally can make other people feel inadequate. (Me, I am other people and, yes, there are times when I feel awkward around him because his kindness is in my face challenging me to be better, to be kinder.) I should, every day strive to find ways that I can be kind and I can serve. You should, too.

Your gesture of kindness doesn't have to be dramatic. To be kind, you just need to, well, be kind! Sometimes it is through service to others that you can truly identify what it feels like to extend true kindness. Service brings awareness to you that the power of being kind is actually inspirational. It is a domino effect, too; Miguel makes me want to be kind. Donating 50 percent of all my proceeds of this book is a kindness. I am lucky because I can afford to do that. We don't have to give away all our money, or all of our time, to be kind. If we can, great! If not, the simple act of offering a dollar to a man on the street or in your barista's tip jar is a kindness. A smile on an elevator is a kindness. Forgiving a friend is a kindness. So let's be kind!

I also say, at all times, be kind to yourself. There is a fine line between being available for a needy friend and being manipulated by them. You must set the boundaries that you will use to offer kindness to others and at the same time honor and be kind to yourself. My friend and I have a great relationship, but I do need to be kind to myself in the relationship, too. I can't have her manipulating me or else it isn't really a friendship anymore, is it. So I place kind invisible boundaries that allow me to continue that friendship, honoring first that those boundaries are my kindness to myself. Being kind does not mean allowing others to walk all over you or take advantage of you. It doesn't mean "be a doormat." In fact, it is the opposite because if your first kindness is always to yourself, you will never be someone's punching bag.

I repeat, kindness does not mean be a sucker! And with that I will end this letter, because my neighbor just blocked me in my driveway and I have to go be kind to them. ☺

Reflections

WHO NEEDS YOUR KINDNESS?
IF YOU CAN'T THINK OF SOMEONE OFF THE
TOP OF YOUR HEAD, PERHAPS YOU CAN DO
AN ONLINE SEARCH FOR "LOCAL VOLUNTEER
OPPORTUNITIES" TO INSPIRE YOU.

YOUR NOVEMBER LETTER
FROM THE PUBLISHER

December

Welcome, December.

WE

*Too often we underestimate the
power of a touch, a smile, a kind word,
a listening ear, an honest compliment, or
the smallest act of caring, all of which have
the potential to turn a life around.*

—Leo Buscaglia

We: *Used by the speaker or writer to indicate the speaker
or writer along with another or others as the subject.*

As a resident of Long Beach, New York, I mentioned earlier that I personally felt the effects of Hurricane Sandy. The lower portion of my home, including basic living utilities, were left in five feet of floodwater and sewage. Everything that was touched by the floodwater needed to be thrown to the curb immediately due to the fear of contamination. We threw away big items, our walls, gas burner, couches, TV, toys, and much more. After hauling out big stuff, all that was left was "little stuff." The doll my sister gave to me when I was ten and she had moved to Texas, our wedding and engagement pictures, our children's footprints from the hospital, even the framed photo of our first "Make a Wish Polar Bear Plunge" (yes, I am one of those crazy people who jump into the ocean in January to raise money for the Make-a-Wish Foundation). Dragging those items, which were left covered in sewage, sand, and water hurt me in a way I will not forget. This loss of "little stuff" caused big pain. I found that I was losing other things during that time, too: my patience, my temper, my control, and my gratitude. The burden I carried was heavy. Even with my husband's help, we felt loaded down.

Yet this letter is not about what I lost, or how heavy the burden was. Honestly, would you read it if it was? I wonder. I mean, loss is not inspiring . . . or is it? In the post-storm days, I learned about the power of "we." As my husband and I were working the pumps to remove water and hauling out twenty years' worth of water-soaked furniture, books, and memories, our driveway began to fill with cars. Words were not even spoken as my husband's friend Phil gave us a hug, put on gloves, and walked down to the basement and began hauling stuff out. My sister and her friends all began showing up with brooms, pails, and bottled water. Her husband, a New York City firefighter, walked into the house after working a twenty-four hour tour and began shoveling sand that was once on the beach and was now a wet, contaminated hill in our basement. Neighbors who had not spoken in months, sometimes years, were respectfully helping carry each other's contents to the curb.

As we cleaned our basement we began to hear tales of people in much worse shape than us, the loss of complete houses, the uninsured, the person who was laid off just days pre-storm. Long Beach residents would spend the next few weeks and months cleaning debris and gutting the houses of neighbors and friends. When we had gotten our house as gutted as possible, we moved to our friends' and neighbors' houses. When that was done, my husband joined a volunteer crew, helping gut houses of people he had never met before. I was witnessing "The Power of We" and it was awe-inspiring!

Then *Natural Awakenings Magazine* advertisers, who had only known me for four weeks, began emailing and calling, offering me office space and a home to live in. I had never even met these people face-to-face, yet they were offering me their home. I was overwhelmed witnessing friends and, more important, strangers coming together to help one another. I witnessed the hope and love of our community, not only Long Beach, but also our entire Long Island community.

While, it's true I lost some stuff, things that were really, really important and that can never be replaced, I gained a profound insight: WE are New Yorkers, WE are Long Islanders, WE are humanity, and together with love WE can rebuild. Together we supported our local businesses and they supported us and we will and are still in the process of building back our little town in the hopes that it will be better than before. And the people of this sleepy beach town I live in are just a little bit closer to one another than we had been prior to "Sandy." We were all changed. Events do that.

I am not the same. I have seen a city I love turned into a pile of debris, and at the same time I have witnessed a community come together to help, and support one another. I am a better person for having been part of that. Perhaps I lost "stuff," but what I gained no flood or hurricane can ever take from me. I gained firsthand the power of WE. WE is stronger than me. WE can get through this. WE love you. WE trumps ME every time! The collective WE that is humanity! Your circle of friends, your family, the WE in your life must be called upon in times of trouble. How truly blessed I feel to have had the opportunity to experience that power of "WE" firsthand.

You don't need a hurricane to make yourself available to the power of WE. There is tremendous joy in helping others. There is also joy in being helped, so seek the power of WE when you are facing a tough time or difficult task. How often do we say, "I've got this!" or "I don't want to be a burden." Think about something you may need help with, then reach out. See how different an experience can be when you are using the power of WE.

Reflections

WHAT DO YOU NEED FROM WE?
IS THERE A WE YOU CAN CONTRIBUTE
YOUR OWN TALENTS TO? GET OUT
THERE AND FIND YOUR TRIBE!

BELIEVE

I've learned to use meditation and relaxation to handle stress. Just kidding, I'm on my third glass of wine.

Believe: *To accept (something) as true; feel sure of the truth of.*

I am almost sad as I come to the end of the book. There are a million words that we can read about, think about, consider, and meditate on. As I thought them through and journaled about them, one that continually made its way to the top was the word "believe."

I was getting nervous, thinking perhaps the beloved word "believe" may not make it in.

For a while, my family knows, believe meant something special. You see, when my sister Diana was dying, she was sick enough to be living in horrendous pain but not sick enough to let go. She absolutely loved this life, so watching her die slowly was like watching someone be dragged out of their own birthday party. And if you knew my sister, you know that she *loved* birthday parties!

It was literally heartbreaking, and most of the time my sisters and I didn't know what to say, not to her and not to each other. We would speak to each other on the phone and I personally clung to a word, *believe*. Diana would say, "I will miss you so much, and the truth is, I don't want to miss you! I want to see you and I want to be with you." What do you say to that? It broke my heart in two. Holding back tears, I said, "I *believe* you won't have to miss me. I think God is good and anywhere he is taking you, well, in some way or form, I believe I will be there with you." It calmed her a bit and I shared that thought with my other sisters. It became our mantra while she was ill. I bought her a shirt, a tank top that had pretty script writing that said, "Believe" on it. She was wearing that shirt the day she finally surrendered.

After Diana died, we equated that word, "believe" to being "her" word. It reminded us of what she needed in the end to let go. Looking back, though, I am unsure if it was her word or ours. I mean, she finally had too much and her soul left. I will never know if, when she left this world, she left believing what I did. I am not sure it matters. *Believe* wasn't really her word or mine; I think it is everyone's word.

Recently, I gave my other sister a bracelet that said "Believe" on it for her birthday. I imagine it made her think of Diana. I was at the counter buying something else for her when I looked to the right of me and saw the bracelet and immediately changed the gift. As I said, Diana loved birthdays and she wasn't missing this one! I do believe that Diana and I were probably together buying the Believe bracelet in some way that none of us can even comprehend. I also believe that when I dream perhaps I go to where she is, although I have only seen her twice in my dreams.

The bracelet I (we) bought, that was for my sister Laura also meant something else to her. Her children are getting older, the business she owns is getting busier, and her life oftentimes seems overwhelming. When I bought the bracelet it was the word I was giving to her and it wasn't really about life or death. *Believe* the bracelet said. Believe that everything happens for a reason. Believe that the struggles you face today will be the memories you learned from yesterday. Believe that, yes, God is good. Believe in God. Believe in yourself. Believe. Believe and it shall be true! Oh, I am not naïve enough to think I can "believe" myself into a size four bikini (and I certainly believe that even if I could, not one of you would want to see it ☺). But still I believe in the simple power of belief.

Belief is this entire book all wrapped up! When "believing," let's not forget it is you who decide what you believe and you who decide how you handle your beliefs. Beliefs can also be a double-edged sword and it is good to take good care of your beliefs.

At the birthday dinner where I gave my sister the bracelet, an argument broke out (actually two). The first argument came about because of a simple discussion about whether it was right or wrong to bring a water bottle (or iced tea) to church. "I believe it is horrible, it is disrespectful!" said one person. "Are you kidding me? Water is fine, if I can't feel comfortable in a home to bring my own water bottle, then I won't go there," said another. Beliefs.

I walked away to the next room and into the next argument, which went something like this: "Fox Five News is the devil, I wouldn't watch that nonsense." This was answered with, "Have you ever even watched it? I believe you probably should actually watch Fox Five News at least once before you criticize it."

Ah belief. It can lead to interesting conversations, that's for sure. I tried to remain neutral. But. It. Is. So. Hard. I have an opinion, a belief, and I began to say it, "My belief is . . ." I should stop there. That's it, my belief. While I would love to have my friends and family come around to my enlightened way of thinking (please note that is said with the belief that you will hear the sarcasm), if you don't come around, so what! For it is simply my belief (and that's good . . . FOR ME . . . shout out to those of you still incorporating the advice months earlier from Panache Desai).

Believe is too strong a word to place on a news channel or an opinion.

Believe should be saved, for something like God, or heaven, or simply when discussing loved ones who you will one day meet again, or who are meeting you daily as you work in your garden, or when you are out buying birthday gifts. Yes, that is what I BELIEVE.

Reflections

DO YOU BELIEVE? IN GOD, IN HEAVEN? IN PEOPLE? WHAT "UNBELIEVABLE" THINGS DO YOU BELIEVE IN?

FAITH

*Faith is the substance of things hoped for,
the evidence of things not seen.*

—Hebrews 11:1

Faith: *Complete trust or confidence in someone or something.*

If I had the power to give everyone a holiday gift, I would give the gift of faith. If accepted, even just by one tenth of one percent of the people on my list, I would know that the gift I gave would rejoice with you when you are happy; sit with you when you are worried; and if you find yourself in a fox hole, I'd like to believe it would be my gift that would be the one thing that would provide you comfort. —me ☺

That was the opening of my December 2013 letter and I was writing it while I was contemplating what gifts I had to run out to buy for the people on my list. The truth came out (as it often does when I put pen to paper) that what I really would love to give people is a strong gift of faith. Gifts as material items don't always make sense to me (unless it is a surfboard, somehow that makes sense to me ☺). Wait, a candle that should have burned for one day burned for eight days, so you should get a present a day? Or, Christ was born so you should get diamonds, pearls, or, for people like me, a new surfboard? Just doesn't compute.

I was speaking with my daughter's friend one day. This little girl has gone through a lot: the loss of her father to a horrifying disease;

Hurricane Sandy, which uprooted her family; and some personal health issues. I mention her background simply because it's important to understand what I'm going to share next. We were talking about life (as us moms sometimes do with these kids), when she mentioned in no uncertain terms, "I am an atheist." She went on to say: "I believe in science!" She continued, "You know, you seem really smart. I am actually surprised that you believe in something like that."

Hmm, I thought to myself. *Something like what? What does she think I believe, simply because I believe in God?* "You know, honey," I responded. "I faced a time when my son was very ill, and the doctors and science couldn't figure it out. Would you believe that at the exact same time, my husband began undergoing tests to diagnosis a rare liver disease that would later turn into an even rarer form of cancer. Science solved both these problems. So, I can certainly see why you believe in science. I do, too. I spent many years in the pharmaceutical and biotech field and my belief in science is strong—almost as strong as my belief in God. Almost. The cure for my husband's condition though—the science—well, it nearly killed him at least four times over a five-year period. It took a very long time for science to come through for me. Faith is not what helped the illnesses," I went on to say. "No way. That was pure and simply skilled surgeons, physicians, and medicine—science. Faith was what helped *me*."

The funny thing is, I get it. When people said to me during those turbulent times, "God doesn't give us more than we can handle," I wanted to vomit or scream. Really? So, there's a guy up there (or Gal) looking through a book saying, "Well, Kelly McGrath Martinsen is of tough Irish and German stock. Let's give her *both* a sick son *and* a sick husband because, well, the lady around the block wouldn't be able to handle it, but good old Kelly can!"?

I have a close friend who was a firefighter in 2001 in New York City. He witnessed the tragedy of 9/11 firsthand, and upon witnessing that complete and utter devastation and evil said, "Right then and there I became an atheist." He questioned further, "How can your God perform selective miracles? Allowing one person to die from cancer while the next survives?" Honestly, I have thought to myself, *If there's a God, then how the heck did those radical assholes take down our Twin Towers, killing all those beautiful people and leaving our first responders still slowly dying to this day?* I get it.

I, too, have doubts, daily, sometimes hourly. Reflecting on my own experience, though, I know it was a *miracle!* No, not my husband's remission; no, that was science. The miracle was that I didn't just curl up in the fetal position and have a nervous breakdown. The only thing that I can attribute that miracle to was the fact that I had my faith; which was the one thing I called on during my darkest hours.

Back to my discussion with my daughter's friend: "So, honey, that is why I'm a bit bummed out by your comment. Not because you no longer think I am smart; I have been called dumb by the best of them. Nah, I am bummed because life is tough, you have already seen that at such a young age, and I am sad that you have no one to yell at, or to blame and to thank, and most of all no one to cry out to and ask for strength."

For some, faith is a "maybe"; for some it's an "absolute"; for some it's a "revolution" or a "cause"; for others, it's a "less-than-1-percent chance." Yet, for all that have even an inkling of faith, it is there when they need it. "I want you to have that there when you need it," I told her.

That conversation impacted me tremendously. If I could give everyone reading this book (assuming again it is more than just my family) a gift, then I would love to offer you the gift of faith. Make it your own imperfect, sometimes doubted, but always there when you need it, faith.

So rather than look for presents for my family and friends on the day I wrote the quote above, I decided instead to write a letter to Santa to see if perhaps he could fill the request list. Here is what I wrote:

Dear Santa,

First, thank you for last year's present! The eight-foot stand-up paddle-surf-board was a great gift, and I loved hitting the ocean this summer and riding waves. I felt like a kid again . . . and it was AWESOME! Speaking of being a kid again, this time of year always reminds me of my childhood when I would eagerly write you a letter with a compilation of all the things that I truly felt I could not live without. Year after year, you came through; not with everything—I see now that would have been gluttonous—but with the really important things. Thanks especially for Christmas 1978; you really hit the nail on the head when you brought me my Lite-Brite!

Santa, we have done this dance countless times, albeit in my younger days, but we both know the routine. I give you a list and you give me the stuff. Right? Nope, not this time around. This year, I am changing it up, Santa. This year, I say, "Keep your stuff." That's right, I said it. Keep. Your. STUFF! I am sick of it. My kids fight over it. It clutters my house, even my mind. So, this year, keep it! Wait, don't just move on to the next "stuff-requesting letter" just yet. I do want to ask for something. Mind you, it's not for me; it's for humanity. You see, Santa, we witness a lot of horrible things each day, and the things we see have me worried. Truly worried. There's disease, war, shootings, terrorism, and words that we weren't even aware of a few years ago, like Ebola and ISIS. Fear not, I am not requesting that you put an end to disease, hunger, or housewives trampling each other to death buying things they think they need, exactly one day after giving thanks for all they had! No, I am realistic and know you can't do that. I know you are just a magic man in a red suit from my childhood who perhaps has not yet taken the self-help steps needed to grab a hold of his own weight problem and trajectory toward self-induced diabetes. The gift that I am putting on my list is a powerful one. This gift will bring a person peace when suffering, courage when attempting, love when questioning, and hope when doubting.

You see, Santa, I got this gift from my parents when I was a little girl; I kept this gift with me throughout my life. Initially, I didn't even take care of it—that happens with gifts when we are young. Truth be told, there were times when I forgot I even had it! Yet I walked around with it day in and day out. It was always with me. I was relieved to discover that after years of not using it, that it still worked. During my darkest hours, when my husband or son was sick or during the tough period when I lost my job, I was very happy to find that it was right where I left it and that without much nurturing at all, it has lasted my entire lifetime and hasn't lost any of its power.

I am talking about Faith. This year, all I want for Christmas is Faith. For those people that already have faith, make it stronger; for those that are struggling to relocate lost faith, make it visible; and here's the tough one: for those folks that have absolutely no faith at all, let them discover it.

That's it. That's all I want for Christmas. I know this whole letter thing is a quid pro quo arrangement, so, in return for granting humanity with the gift of faith—renewed, stronger, or new—you will get one nice glass of organic milk; three homemade sugar-free, gluten-free Paleo cookies (I can't promise they will taste good); and some kale for your reindeer. What do you think? Is it a deal?

Reflections

WHERE DOES YOUR FAITH LIE?
IN WHOM DO YOU HAVE FAITH?

_____
_____
_____
_____
_____
_____
_____
_____
_____
_____
_____
_____
_____
_____
_____
_____
_____
_____
_____
_____
_____
_____

YOUR DECEMBER
LETTER FROM THE PUBLISHER

Afterword

Your year is complete, mine, too. Was there a word or a particular month that resonated with you as an area that you wanted to focus on? One thing grabbed hold for me when writing this book: I found myself sharing my thoughts and ideas with my kids (they *really* loved the whole "Thank-You Experiment") so I am going to pursue the development of *A Year of Inspired Living for Teens.* I am excited to work through this book a second time, incorporating much smaller chapters *and* figuring out how to get it on Snapchat (I mean seriously I doubt they will read it if I don't ☺).

A really big month for me turned out to be December. The faith chapter was literally like twenty pages prior to cutting it down. There was so much I could say about it, so much I had heard and witnessed about the value of faith in both good times and bad. Faith, well, it sort of took hold, not in a conversion type banging on doors, handing out pamphlets sort of way, but in a way that made me think, *Imagine if I focused on a year of faithful living.* This thought has inspired me to continue my writing journey and I hope you will all join me in my next yearlong adventure when I share with you *A Year of Faithful Living.* Finding faith in good and bad times.

What about you? Did this year of inspiration take hold and change something for you? Are you being more kind, less angry? Are you evolving in your existing relationship rather than looking to fall in love with someone new? Are you reframing the bad occurrences in your life so that you aren't viewing yourself as a victim? How about playing? Have you joined a team or taken a surfing lesson? I really pray that this book opened space in your life for some transformation and that you take the things that surfaced for you into the next year, and the year after that. In the end, I hope that every year you live will be an inspired one. I also invite you to join me on my journey of inspired living and follow me on my website, kellymcgrathmartinsen.com and on my Facebook page, Author Kelly Martinsen.

The happiest people don't have everything they just make the best of everything.

—*Unknown*

Acknowledgments

This book is dedicated to my husband Kevin (there is no one in the world that I would rather search for inspiration with!) and my children, Dylan and Reagan, whose smiles are my reason for living. My mother and father Ray and Marilyn McGrath, I love you both so much, thank you for making me believe that I could succeed at anything! My sisters who know me so well, and who put up with my crankiness, who love to laugh with me and who accept that I can't cry in front of people; they are my best friends. My in-laws Dan and Betty Martinsen, whose excitement for this book kept me writing on days I didn't want to. My sisters- and brothers-in-law, nieces and nephews (even my furry ones). My neighbors, my friends, my #lafamilia, my "running box girls" who saved me tons of money on therapy just by running those long miles with me. My "soul sisters" and my entire Long Beach, New York, community. Without these people I am not sure this book would have been published.

Three days before the final edit was to go to my publisher, I had a house fire. It was three o'clock in the morning and we had friends in the guest bedroom who smelled the smoke. Waleka and her son Gian woke us and they will forever be my angels here on Earth. We were all able to run out of the house to safety. We survived, the house did not. In the days that followed, my family, neighbors, and friends saved me from a fate worse than a destroyed home and all its memories . . . they saved me from being engulfed in despair. Within hours of the fire being put out, and continuing throughout the week, people arrived at my home offering clothes, food, a place to stay and, most importantly, hugs. If you are one of those people who reached out via text or Facebook, phone or email, who offered me your home, your clothes, food, hugs, love, or any kindness during that time, please know I appreciate you! I have no idea what I would have done without these people in my life. This book is dedicated to their charity, love, and truly inspiring behavior.